○ **Collins** · NATURE GUIDE

WHALES &
DOLPHINS

WRITTEN AND PHOTOGRAPHED

BY

MARK CARWARDINE

Collins

Reprinted in 2012 for
Independent Book Sales

*For Mum and Dad – thank you for your endless love, support
and encouragement.*

HarperCollins Publishers
77-85 Fulham Palace Road
London
W6 8JB

www.collins.co.uk

Collins is a registered trademark of HarperCollins Publishers Ltd.

First published in 2006

Text © 2006 Mark Carwardine
Artworks © Martin Camm/www.markcarwardine.com
Images © Mark Carwardine, except p. 233, © Florian
Gramer/Nature PL

12

10 9 8 7 6 5 4 3 2

ISBN: 978 0 00 786714 1

Editor: Emily Pitcher
Commissioning Editor: Helen Brocklehurst
Designer: Martin Brown
Proofreader: Claire Wedderburn-Maxwell
Index: Lisa Foottit

Colour reproduction by Colourscan, Singapore
Printed and bound in China by South China Printing Company

CONTENTS

INTRODUCTION

There is something special about whales, dolphins and porpoises. They are still shrouded in mystery, yet the little we do know about them is both astonishing and awe-inspiring. They include the largest animal on Earth, the deepest-diving mammal, the mammal with the longest known migration, species that are capable of emitting the loudest sounds in nature, and many other extraordinary creatures. They also include some of the world's most critically endangered species.

Watching them in the wild is probably the ultimate wildlife experience. Once you have met a whale, dolphin or porpoise face-to-face, life is never quite the same again. There is an immense and lasting satisfaction in simply knowing that it is out there, wild and free. Who could ever forget the sight of a 50-tonne southern right whale launching itself high into the air, or of a sperm whale diving into the cold, dark depths hundreds or even thousands of metres below the surface? Who could fail to be intrigued

Short-beaked common dolphin, Sea of Cortez, Mexico

Southern right whales, Western Cape, South Africa

by Bahamonde's beaked whale, which is known from only two partial skulls, an old tooth and a lower jaw, or remain untouched by the plight of the last few surviving Yangtze river dolphins?

It is not surprising that every year more than 10 million people join organised whale and dolphin watching trips, in at least 87 different countries and overseas territories around the world.

The aim of this book is to introduce the world of whales, dolphins and porpoises and to provide a handy pocket guide for use in the field. It includes information on their evolution, biology and natural history, describes how they are studied, the threats they face, and some of the efforts to protect the ones most in trouble. But most of all it provides a comprehensive directory of all 84 currently-recognised species – and a few more that could become distinct species in the future. I hope it will help you to find, recognise, watch, enjoy and respect whales, dolphins and porpoises in the wild.

THE NATURAL HISTORY OF WHALES, DOLPHINS AND PORPOISES

Evolution

The broad outline of the evolution of whales, dolphins and porpoises is quite well-known, but there are still many gaps in our knowledge. Tiny fragments – a few teeth or miniscule pieces of bone – sometimes provide the only tantalising clues to important links in their evolutionary chain.

They are believed to have evolved from a group of furry land mammals called mesonychids. These strange creatures looked rather like wolves, with four legs and a tail, but had hooves – so whales and hoofed animals such as hippos and deer appear to have a common ancestor. They lived around the ancient Tethys Sea, an area that is now the Mediterranean Sea and part of the Asian sub-continent, about 55–60 million years ago. The mesonychids probably

Mesonychid

spent their lives foraging for fish and other aquatic animals in coastal swamps and estuaries. As they spent more and more time in the water their bodies began to change. They became more streamlined and developed powerful, flattened tails; their forelimbs gradually turned into paddles and their hindlimbs wasted away; they developed insulating layers of fat and their body hair began to disappear; and, to help them breathe at the surface, their nostrils started to move towards the top of their heads to become blowholes.

It is still possible to see evidence of these land-based ancestors in modern whales, dolphins and porpoises. Intriguingly, the bone structure of the pectoral fin, or flipper, closely resembles an arm and hand with fingers; and, trapped inside the blubber, are the remains of pelvic bones that millions of years ago held their hindlimbs.

The first real whale-like animals appeared about 10 million years later. These ancient whales, or archaeocetes, spread rapidly throughout the oceans of the world – their fossilised remains have been found as far afield as Britain, Canada, Australia and even Antarctica. They were probably very similar to modern whales, dolphins and porpoises, although they were less well-adapted to life in the sea. They may even have clambered back onto land to breed, just like modern seals.

For reasons that are unclear the last of the archaeocetes probably died out about 25–30 million years ago but, by this time, representatives of more modern whales, dolphins and porpoises were fairly common and widespread. None were exactly the same as the species alive today, but they were unmistakably similar in appearance and way of life. The split between toothed whales (odontocetes) and baleen whales (mysticetes) occurred some 25–35 million years ago and by about five million years ago most, if not all, modern families of whales, dolphins and porpoises had become firmly established.

Archaeocete

Diversity

The sheer diversity of whales, dolphins and porpoises tends to surprise many people. A few species, such as the killer whale, narwhal and bottlenose dolphin, are relatively well-known. But the vast majority go unnoticed by all but the most dedicated whale-watchers.

In fact, there are currently no fewer than 84 recognised species altogether and, as research progresses, new discoveries continue to be made and the total count slowly but surely increases. A new species of beaked whale, Perrin's beaked whale, was formally recognised as recently as 2002 and the latest genetic research is revealing that some animals previously thought to be single species should actually be 'split'. In 1995, for example, the common dolphin was officially separated into two distinct species, now known as the short-beaked common dolphin and the long-beaked common dolphin. In the late 1990s, the minke whale was split into the common minke and the Antarctic minke and, in the future, it is possible that a third species – the dwarf minke – could be declared.

There is also some debate about Bryde's whales. A pygmy form will likely be assigned separate species status in the near future and, according to recent evidence from Japan, a third species is also possible. In the late 1970s, eight unidentified

Spinner dolphin, The Maldives

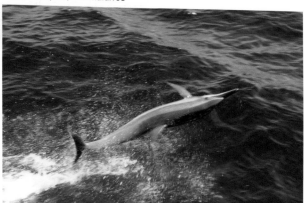

baleen whales were caught in the Indo-Pacific by Japanese whalers – and, in 1998, a ninth specimen was found beached on an island in the Sea of Japan. They all resembled fin whales, but were much smaller and had slightly unusual skulls and a different number of baleen plates. Genetic studies group all nine animals together as a single species, but separate them from all known baleen whale species.

While all these animals share many characteristics, there is no 'typical' whale, dolphin or porpoise. In size alone, they range from tiny dolphins and porpoises just over one metre long, to whales that are known to reach lengths of more than 33 metres. In terms of weight, the heaviest species is no less than 3,000 times heavier than the lightest.

They abound in an amazing variety of different shapes as well. Some are long and slender, others short and stocky. Some have huge dorsal fins, others have no fins at all. Many are brightly coloured or striking in black and white, while others are rather drab.

They also have a range of different habits and lifestyles. Some live in freezing cold waters near the poles, others prefer the warmer waters of the tropics. Many live in the middle of the deepest oceans, but others prefer to be much closer to shore, while a few even live hundreds of kilometres inland in rivers such as the Yangtze, the Ganges and the Amazon.

Humpback whale, Monterey Bay, USA

Is it a whale, a dolphin, or a porpoise?

Whales, dolphins and porpoises are known collectively as cetaceans. They form the largest of the three main groups of marine mammals surviving today, the others being the pinnipeds (seals, sea lions and walrus) and the sirenians (sea cows or manatees and dugong).

Interestingly, there is no real scientific basis for splitting cetaceans into the three groups commonly known as 'whales', 'dolphins' and 'porpoises'. Broadly speaking, the word 'whale' is used to describe the largest animals, 'dolphin' to describe the medium-sized ones, and 'porpoise' to describe the smallest. But this can be misleading, since some whales are smaller than the largest dolphins, and some dolphins are smaller than the largest porpoises.

There are many more confusing names and terms, as well. The rightwhale dolphins, for example, were named after right whales but are actually dolphins. At the same time, many are known by umpteen different names in at least as many different languages. Thus the northern giant bottlenose whale, North Pacific bottlenose whale, giant four-toothed whale, northern four-toothed whale and Baird's beaked whale are all the same species.

Melon-headed whales, The Maldives

Even more confusing are six members of the dolphin family, the Delphinidae, which have the word 'whale' in their names: killer whale, pygmy killer whale, false killer whale, melon-headed whale, long-finned pilot whale and short-finned pilot whale. These six species are often classified together in a group known as the 'blackfish', which is also rather strange since not all of them are black and, of course, none is a fish.

Scientists prefer to split modern cetaceans into just two distinct groups: the toothed whales, or Odontocetes, and the baleen whales, or Mysticetes. There was also a third group, known as the ancient whales or Archaeocetes, but all its members have been extinct for millions of years.

As their name suggests, the toothed whales possess teeth; this group of 71 species includes all the beaked whales, sperm whales, blackfish, oceanic dolphins, river dolphins and porpoises. The baleen whales make up the remaining 13 species and, instead of teeth, have hundreds of strange-looking baleen plates hanging down from their upper jaws; they make up for their lack of numbers by including most of the larger and better-known whales, including the blue, humpback, grey and right whales.

Inside and out

Whales, dolphins and porpoises are so streamlined, and so well adapted to life underwater, that they look rather like sharks and other large fish. They even have similar dorsal fins, flippers and powerful tails. But appearances can be deceptive. The similarities between them are simply the result of two unrelated groups of animals adapting in similar ways to identical living conditions. On closer inspection, there are actually more differences between them than there are similarities.

In particular, fish are cold-blooded, use their gills to extract all the oxygen they need directly from the water, and normally lay eggs or give birth to young that can feed themselves. In contrast, whales, dolphins and porpoises are mammals, like us, and so are warm-blooded, breathe air with lungs, and give birth to young that feed on their mother's milk for the first weeks or months of life.

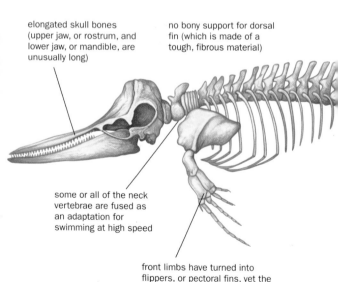

elongated skull bones (upper jaw, or rostrum, and lower jaw, or mandible, are unusually long)

no bony support for dorsal fin (which is made of a tough, fibrous material)

some or all of the neck vertebrae are fused as an adaptation for swimming at high speed

front limbs have turned into flippers, or pectoral fins, yet the original structure of the arm, hand and finger bones is still visible

One of the most striking features of any cetacean is the thick layer of insulating fat under the skin, known as blubber, which they have instead of hair or fur. This helps them to keep warm in water, which sucks heat out of a mammal up to 25 times faster than in air.

A detailed look inside their bodies reveals many other interesting features and adaptations for their underwater life:

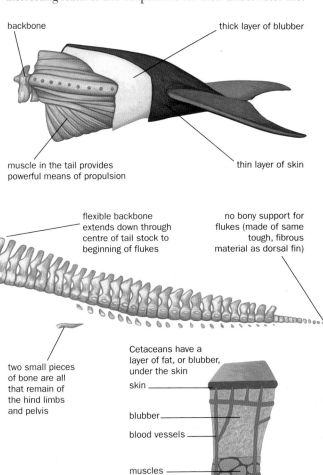

backbone

thick layer of blubber

muscle in the tail provides powerful means of propulsion

thin layer of skin

flexible backbone extends down through centre of tail stock to beginning of flukes

no bony support for flukes (made of same tough, fibrous material as dorsal fin)

two small pieces of bone are all that remain of the hind limbs and pelvis

Cetaceans have a layer of fat, or blubber, under the skin

skin

blubber

blood vessels

muscles

Diving and swimming

The fastest speed ever achieved by a human swimmer is an incredible 8.64 km/h by American Tom Jager, on 23 March 1990 in Nashville, USA. Equally impressive, the record depth attained for no-limits freediving is 209 metres, achieved by Belgian Patrick Musimu on 30 June 2005, in the Red Sea. And on 8 November 2003, Frenchman Stephane Mifsud held his breath for a record-breaking eight minutes 24 seconds.

But these superhuman feats barely register on the scale of the swimming and diving records achieved by whales, dolphins and porpoises. Killer whales, Dall's porpoises and several other species have been clocked at speeds of up to 55 km/h, while sperm whales (and, possibly, some beaked whales) can dive to depths of at least 2,000 metres and have been known to stay underwater for nearly two hours at a time.

All cetaceans are proficient swimmers and divers, even though they breathe air and, consequently, have to hold their breath whenever they disappear underwater. Their lungs are relatively small, but they are able to extract much more oxygen from the air than human lungs and then use it far more efficiently.

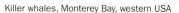

Killer whales, Monterey Bay, western USA

Avoiding the 'bends': Human scuba divers can suffer from a potentially fatal condition known as decompression sickness, or the 'bends'. It is caused by nitrogen bubbling out of the blood, either when the divers stay down for too long or when they rise to the surface too quickly. These bubbles then lodge in joints and cause severe pain, or in vital blood vessels and cause paralysis or even death.

Marine biologists have always assumed that cetaceans are immune to the bends, but now it seems that rising to the surface too quickly from deep water may be just as dangerous for them as it is for us. Damage consistent with decompression sickness has been found in the bones of sperm whales and beaked whales.

Humpback whale, Silver Bank, Dominican Republic

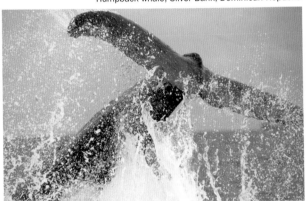

Avoiding 'nitrogen narcosis': On deep dives, human scuba divers can suffer from another dangerous condition called 'nitrogen narcosis'. They start losing control over what they are doing and their judgement begins to deteriorate, as if they are drunk. In a way, they behave like car drivers under the influence of alcohol because, although nitrogen narcosis is not dangerous in itself, it makes accidents far more likely.

Whales, dolphins and porpoises do not suffer from nitrogen narcosis either, because it is induced by breathing nitrogen under pressure – and they breathe it only at the surface.

Food and feeding

Most whales, dolphins and porpoises feed on fish, squid or crustaceans, but some will take a wide variety of other prey as well – at virtually every level in the marine ecosystem – ranging from octopuses to other large whales.

Between them, they have an astonishing range of different hunting techniques. For example, killer whales in Patagonia will beach themselves to catch sea lion pups; strap-toothed whales suck squid into their mouths so quickly that the squid appear to have been attached to pieces of invisible elastic; belugas blast powerful jets of water to dislodge fish hiding in mud on the seabed; open-ocean dolphins work together to corral fish against the surface of the sea; and blue whales take huge quantities of water into their mouths, and then filter out as much as four tonnes of shrimp-like krill every day.

In turn, they themselves are preyed upon by large sharks and even by some of their own kind: killer whales, false killer whales and pygmy killer whales. The smaller species are most at risk, but no whale is too large for a determined pod of killer whales.

Teeth: As their name suggests, all toothed whales have teeth. But the number varies greatly from species to species and, in some female beaked whales, they have no visible teeth at all (they do not erupt). Cetacean teeth come in a variety of shapes and sizes, but in most cases each species has just one design – in other words, they are not differentiated into incisors, canines, pre-molars and molars. Unlike other mammals, toothed whales do not have two sets of teeth, but retain their first set for life.

Sperm whale   Ginkgo-toothed   Fraser's
beaked whale   Dolphin

Baleen plates: Instead of teeth, most large whales have hundreds of strange-looking structures hanging down from their upper jaws. These are called baleen plates. They overlap one another, inside the mouth, to form bristly sieves for filtering small animals out of the seawater. Some 400–700 baleen plates is typical for most whales, but their number, size and shape varies greatly from species to species.

Bowhead   Fin   Minke

Krill: Krill are small, shrimp-like crustaceans, known in the scientific world as euphausiids. Full of protein, and living in dense swarms, they make ideal food for large whales. There are at least 80 different species of krill, ranging in length from eight to 60 millimetres, but perhaps the most important is the five- to six-centimetre Antarctic krill. This is the staple food of all baleen whales in the Antarctic, as well as fish, squid, penguins and seals.

Migration

Many large baleen whales have little choice but to split their year into four distinct parts. They spend a few months, in the summer, gorging themselves on schooling fish and krill, in high-latitude, cold water feeding grounds; in the autumn, they migrate to low-latitude, warm water breeding grounds; then they spend a few months, during the winter, mating and calving; and finally, in the spring, they migrate all the way back to their feeding grounds, and the annual cycle begins all over again.

The problem they face is that most of their food is in colder regions, in temperate latitudes and towards the sub-Arctic and the Antarctic. In an ideal world, this is where they would live year-round. Unfortunately, though, the food is only present in large quantities during the summer and, even if they stayed for the winter to breed, their newborn calves may not be able to survive the freezing cold temperatures. In other words, their preferred feeding and breeding grounds can be thousands of kilometres apart.

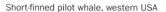

Short-finned pilot whale, western USA

Researchers studying whale migration have made some incredible discoveries in recent years. Some humpback whales, for example, swim between their feeding grounds near the Antarctic Peninsula and their breeding grounds off the coast of Colombia every year – an astonishing round-trip of 17,400 kilometres. Another humpback whale was recorded swimming all the way across the North Pacific, from south-east Alaska to Hawaii, in just 39 days.

But in most cases the more subtle details of their migrations are still a mystery. How do they know when to leave, and when to return? How do they find their way? Do they stop to rest, or feed? Do they swim near the surface, or travel at depth? There are so many unanswered questions.

Not all large baleen whales undertake these extensive migrations. Many Bryde's and minke whales are able to live in non-extreme temperatures year-round, while sei whales, and some humpbacks and greys, do not bother to complete their journeys if they find adequate food supplies en route. Fin whales in Mexico's Sea of Cortez, and blue whales in the northern Indian Ocean, seem to be permanent residents, while bowhead whales simply move backwards and forwards in their high Arctic home, with the advancing and retreating ice.

Blue whale, Sea of Cortez, Mexico

Regular long-distance migrations are virtually unknown in toothed whales, with one major exception. While female and young sperm whales spend most of their lives in warm waters, many of the older males are believed to move to rich feeding grounds, in high-latitude cold waters, during the spring and summer.

Nursing: It is believed that the father plays no active role in caring for the calf, so it is the mother's responsibility alone. Suckling takes place underwater, and she literally squirts her rich, fat-laden milk into the young animal's mouth. The calf grows quickly. A young blue whale, for example, grows almost four centimetres and gains 90 kilograms every day – equivalent to the weight of an average adult man. Weaning is usually gradual, with a period of overlap when the calf is drinking milk and eating solid food at the same time. It stays with its mother for weeks, months or even years afterwards, depending on the species. In general, toothed whales tend to have fewer young and look after them for a relatively long time, whereas baleen whales have more young and look after them for a relatively short time.

Lifespan: It is difficult to assess the ages of whales, dolphins and porpoises accurately and the maximum lifespan for most species is unknown. However, the limited information available suggests that the larger whales tend to have the longest lifespans – probably well in excess of 100 years in the bowhead whale and some others. Certain dolphins and porpoises may have an average life-expectancy of less than 20 years. The two main natural causes of death are predation and disease. A variety of accidents and, of course, human-induced deaths also take their toll.

Social life: Whales, dolphins and porpoises often have complex social lives and have adopted many different ways of living together. Some prefer to live alone, or in small groups, while others roam the seas in the company of hundreds or thousands of their contemporaries. Historically, there are even records of dolphin schools at least 100,000-strong. Some species, such as killer whales and long-finned pilot whales, live in groups that are stable for many years – they remain together for the entire lives of the individuals in them. Others are incredibly fluid and their membership changes all the time, with individuals coming and going quite freely. Often, the membership of a group will vary according to specific requirements on a day-by-day or even hour-by-hour basis.

Commonly asked questions

How intelligent are they?

Are whales, dolphins and porpoises as intelligent as we would like to believe? They certainly *seem* to be intelligent: they have large brains, frequently live in complex societies, help one another in times of trouble, learn from experience, are often playful, and sometimes even seem to enjoy human company. But, in truth, no one really knows. Some people claim that they are no more intelligent than cats and dogs, while others go so far as to say that they may be our intellectual superiors.

There are two main reasons for this confusion. The first lies in defining what we mean by 'intelligent' and then taking meaningful measurements. Many definitions have been proposed over the years, but intelligence is broadly considered to be an ability to learn from experience and then to analyse new situations, rather than simply reacting to

Friendly bottlenose dolphin with swimmer, Kaikoura, New Zealand them. In other words, intelligent animals are able to *solve* problems by grasping fundamental principles, and then making considered judgements, rather than fumbling around trying to get things right by trial and error. Even with an acceptable definition, though, obtaining accurate measurements is another matter altogether. It is hard enough in humans, because the results can be frustratingly ambiguous and difficult to understand. But it is even more challenging in other animals, which cannot talk or work with tools such as pens or computers.

The second reason is that any discussion of intelligence tends to be highly subjective. After all, we have only a human perspective, and can scarcely imagine what goes on inside another animal's mind. Even by saying that a whale or dolphin is more intelligent than, say, a rat or a chicken, we impose a very egocentric set of values and rules.

The simple fact that whales, dolphins and porpoises have embarked on a completely different evolutionary path from our own makes any comparison almost impossible. Human intelligence suits our own way of life and, consequently, a large part of our brain deals with the use of hands to write, paint, sculpt, build or manipulate objects that exist outside our own bodies.

If we were to judge whales and dolphins on these terms, they would fare badly. But their intelligence suits a completely different way of life, and may concentrate instead on social skills, emotional self-control and other more spiritual and philosophical requirements. Taking this into consideration, many people would argue that whales and dolphins are far more intelligent in their world than we are in ours. But the jury is still out.

Why do they strand?

Every year, hundreds or even thousands of whales, dolphins and porpoises are found stranded on coastlines all over the world. They may be alive or dead, alone or in groups, and healthy or unwell. These strandings are believed to be a natural phenomenon (although, in modern times, pollution and acoustic disturbance may be contributory causes in some areas) and have probably been happening for thousands of years. But *why* they happen remains one of the great unsolved mysteries of the animal kingdom.

Strandings of dead animals are relatively easy to explain – they simply die at sea and are washed ashore with the tides and currents – and live animals often strand because they are very ill. But mass strandings of otherwise healthy animals are more baffling. Many theories have been suggested, ranging from severe weather (quite possible) to mass suicide bids (highly unlikely).

But recent research implies that it could be storms exploding from the sun that are making the whales run aground. Historical records of sperm whales found beached in the North Sea, over a 300-year period, show an amazing match with the number of 'sunspots' that blast electrical energy into space. This smashes into the earth's magnetic field (which the whales may use for navigation) and disrupts their internal compasses.

In reality, of course, there may be different explanations for different strandings, depending on the species, location and a variety of other factors.

Stranded sperm whale,
Horta, Faial, The Azores

What should you do if you find a stranded animal?

Without human intervention, when a live whale, dolphin or porpoise strands it usually dies. Cetaceans are not adapted to life on land – they quickly overheat and, out of the relatively weightless medium of the sea, their light bones cannot support their bodies and they literally crush themselves to death. Rescuing a stranded animal is extremely difficult and normally requires great skill and patience. Well-intentioned, but misdirected, efforts can cause considerable stress to the animal and may even result in its death. It can also be quite dangerous to attempt a rescue, since even small cetaceans have been known to injure human helpers when they thrash around. Perhaps not surprisingly, in some countries it is illegal to give unauthorised first aid to any stranded cetacean.

These very basic guidelines are designed merely to make a stranded animal as comfortable as possible until expert help arrives. The golden rule in every case is to call the local police immediately and to attempt a rescue yourself only if expert help is unavailable.

■ Try to keep the animal upper-side up, taking care not to trap either of the flippers under its body, and never pushing or pulling on the flippers, flukes or head.

■ Keep the animal's skin moist and cool, with wet towels or water, but be careful not to cover the blowhole (or to let either water or sand enter the blowhole).

■ Erect a shelter to provide shade from the sun, but never apply suntan lotion to the animal's skin.

■ Keep onlookers and their dogs at a distance, make as little noise as possible, and do not touch the animal more than necessary.

■ Never, under any circumstances, attempt to destroy a stranded animal yourself.

Spinner dolphin which died
after stranding,
Sri Lanka

How do they sleep?

The way in which whales, dolphins and porpoises sleep has
baffled and intrigued scientists for a very long time. Aristotle
seemed particularly excited, centuries ago, when he noted
that 'there are even people who have heard a dolphin snore'.

Over the years, of course, there have been some
interesting theories. One was that they haul themselves out
of the sea after dark and then spend the night curled up on
shore in the company of seals and sea lions; no-one had
actually seen them doing it, but the idea probably seemed
quite logical at the time. Another theory was that they simply
dive down to the seabed, make themselves comfortable, and
lie there for the night.

In fact, the truth is even stranger than the fiction. Unlike
most other mammals, cetaceans never fall into a deep sleep,
and they do not seem to have regular sleeping patterns
linked to night and day. They do sleep, of course, though not
in the way we might expect.

The reason is simple. Since our breathing is automatic, we can safely sleep and breathe at the same time. But cetaceans control their breathing consciously, so they have to be awake, and able to think, in order to take regular breaths. If they were to fall into a deep sleep, which is a naturally-occurring state of unconsciousness, they would then drown.

Keiko, a captive killer whale used in the *Free Willy* films, Oregon, USA

Instead of long periods of deep sleep, their solution is to swim along slowly, or lie just below the surface, and take short 'cat-naps'. They are believed to go into a semi-conscious state by switching off one half of the brain at a time. Then they swap sides to ensure that both halves are fully rested. While one side of the brain is asleep, the other remains awake to control the breathing and, of course, to look out for predators.

Should they be kept in captivity?

During the past century, more than 25 species of whales, dolphins and porpoises have been kept in captivity in zoos, marine parks and aquaria around the world. Thousands of individual animals have been captured in the wild, sometimes for research or military purposes, but mainly to perform special shows for the fee-paying public. They are trained to jump through hoops, balance balls on their heads, 'kiss' their trainers, perform somersaults and synchronised leaps, and to do many other tricks for the millions of people who flock to see them every year.

Their owners argue that the animals 'enjoy' the shows, and are fortunate to be safe from predators, pollution and other threats in the wild. They point out that, as the undisputed stars of zoos and marine parks, they are worth a great deal of money and, directly or indirectly, provide thousands of people with secure jobs. They also claim that captive animals encourage members of the public to take an interest in the conservation of their wild relatives.

Some facilities are obviously much better than others, and whales and dolphins are kept in a bewildering range of establishments, from dirty hotel pools to professional marine parks with large, coastal enclosures that are filled naturally with seawater and flushed with every new tide. Many of the animals are treated abominably, while a very lucky few receive the best care and attention that money can buy.

But most conservation and animal welfare groups are strongly opposed to keeping whales, dolphins or porpoises in captivity of any kind. They say that it is immoral and cruel. Taken from the wild, and separated from their well-structured family groups, the animals are often forced to live alone or with unfamiliar species. Many of them are kept in small and featureless concrete tanks, where they can no longer hunt or hear the sounds of the sea, and may even be deprived of natural sunlight. At the same time, they have to eat dead fish and cope with hordes of noisy people watching them day after day.

To make matters worse, few zoos or marine parks make a genuine effort to educate the public, or 'educate' them with inaccurate information, so the real benefits and spin-offs for their wild relatives are very limited. At the end of the day, there is little doubt that most captive animals are there simply to provide cheap entertainment for profit.

Will we ever be able to talk to them?

Whales, dolphins and porpoises are known to communicate in two main ways: by sound and with body language. They may even be telepathic, as well, and thus able to communicate without speech or movement.

But current evidence suggests that they probably do not have a true language. While they can pass on information such as danger, irritation or sexual interest, they probably cannot complain about the poor size of fish, discuss the vagaries of the weather, or talk about their plans for the future. In other words, they can give simple commands and signals, but probably cannot discuss more abstract concepts.

However, there is no doubt that we still have a great deal to learn about their communication skills. Some dolphins, for example, seem to have their own 'signature whistles', which are almost the equivalent of human names. They use these to attract the attention of other dolphins and to identify themselves; there is even some evidence to suggest that one dolphin will call the name of another in its group.

In captivity, research also demonstrates that they can grasp the essential elements of any human language. They do not actually speak, of course, but they can respond correctly to sentences up to five words long. This suggests that they have the *potential* to develop a language, even if they have not done so in the wild.

Humpback whale watchers, eastern USA

Whether or not we will ever be able to communicate with them is another matter altogether. In the past, people predicted that we would be conversing with dolphins, and other small cetaceans, within a few decades; others went so far as to suggest that if an alien intelligence were to attempt to communicate with life on Earth, it might choose dolphins in preference to humans. But these are dreams that have yet to come true.

How do they find their way around?

Whales, dolphins and porpoises find their way around their underwater world in ways that are well beyond the scope of our own senses. Most of them retain the senses of sight, touch and taste, but they rely mainly on hearing. They are also believed to have an extra sense, known as geomagnetism, which enables them to detect the Earth's magnetic field.

The ability to see varies greatly from one species to another. While some of the river dolphins are virtually blind, for example, most

Killer whale, northern Norway

marine cetaceans can see fairly well in both air and water. However, sight is of limited benefit to them since they spend so much of their lives in the dark depths or in turbid water where visibility is poor even close to the surface.

Hearing is far more important. Effective at night as well as during the day, it does not rely on good visibility. Sound travels through water nearly five times faster than through air and can be heard over much longer distances. Although cetaceans have lost the distinctive outer ear flaps typical of most other mammals, they do have ears in the form of tiny holes in the skin behind their eyes. Many species can probably also receive sounds through their lower jaws.

The senses of taste and smell are very similar, because they are both used to detect chemicals. It is possible to smell underwater: sharks, for example, can smell chemicals in the water from a long distance away. But toothed whales have probably lost their sense of smell altogether, and baleen whales retain only a rudimentary form – mainly because their nostrils (or blowholes) have to remain tightly shut when they dive. Taste is far more important and is used for detecting chemicals both inside and near the outside of the mouth.

Whales, dolphins and porpoises also have very sensitive skin and are able to use their dorsal fins, flippers and beaks to investigate unfamiliar objects, and to touch one another as a form of greeting, or to strengthen social bonds.

Geomagnetism is undoubtedly the least known of all the senses. It involves detecting or 'reading' the Earth's magnetic field, possibly using it like an invisible 'map' to navigate over large distances. Many animals, from bacteria and bees to reptiles and birds, are believed to have this sixth sense. It may even exist to a limited degree in humans – what we identify in ourselves simply as a 'sense of direction'. But it seems to be particularly well developed in many cetaceans, and may help them to navigate their way across the world's seas and oceans.

Whales and dolphins are believed to 'read' the Earth's magnetic field like an invisible 'map'.

What is echolocation?

Most whales, dolphins and porpoises have a remarkable sensory system, called echolocation, which enables them to build up a 'picture' of their underwater surroundings with the help of sound. Bats, shrews, cave swiftlets, oilbirds and a number of other land-based animals use a similar system to hunt fast-moving prey in the dark.

The basic principle of the echolocation system used by cetaceans is quite simple: they transmit ultrasonic clicks into the water, and then monitor and interpret any echoes that bounce back. The clicks are believed to be produced within the nasal plugs, or in the larynx, and are then focused into a directional beam by the fatty 'melon' (which appears as a rounded forehead on most species). The returning echoes may be picked up by the small ear holes on either side of the head, but recent research suggests that they are more likely to be transmitted to the brain via the lower jaw.

Echolocation is actually a form of sonar (radar works in a similar way, but uses electromagnetic radiation instead of sound). However, the system used by many cetaceans is so complex and sophisticated that it leaves human sonar experts gasping: the human system, although useful, is little more than a

Common dolphin, Mexico

crude imitation by comparison. When homing in on a fish, for example, a dolphin can use echolocation to identify the fish's size and shape, which way it is swimming, its texture, and possibly even its internal structure.

Toothed whales are the real echolocation experts. They use it for keeping track of one another, navigating around objects in the water, identifying changes in sea-floor profile, hunting, and monitoring the surroundings for potential predators or prey. It is even possible that some toothed whales may be able to use particularly powerful blasts of ultrasonic clicks to stun or kill their prey. Baleen whales may also be able to echolocate, but this has never been proven and any sonar system they do have is probably much less well-developed. How baleen whales find their food is still largely a mystery.

Echolocation at work

Record-breakers

Largest: The blue whale is the largest animal on Earth. The average adult length is 25 metres in males and 26.2 metres in females, with body weights of 90–120 tonnes. The heaviest ever recorded was a female, caught in the Southern Ocean on 20 March 1947, which weighed 190 tonnes. The longest ever recorded was another female, landed in 1909 at Grytviken, South Georgia, in the South Atlantic, which measured 33.58 metres from the tip of her snout to the end of her tail.

Blue whale, Sea of Cortez, Mexico

Smallest: It is very difficult to identify the world's smallest cetacean, partly because there is so much variation between individuals. Taking the maximum known length as a guide, it is a competition between Hector's dolphin (1.38 metres for the smaller male) and the vaquita (1.45 metres also for the smaller male).

Longest flippers: The longest flippers belong to the humpback whale. They grow to 23–31 per cent of the length of the whale – making a potential maximum of over 5.5 metres – but typically measure around 4.6 metres in fully grown animals. They are used to herd fish, to manoeuvre while swimming, to comfort their young and to slap the surface of the water.

Humpback whale, New England, USA

Tallest dorsal fin: The huge, triangular dorsal fin of the
bull killer whale can reach a remarkable height of 1.8 metres,
which makes it roughly as tall as a man. In comparison, the
blue whale's dorsal fin is relatively small, rarely reaching
more than 40 centimetres in height.

Longest baleen plate: The longest baleen is found in the
bowhead whale. There are many records within the three to
four metre range, but lengths of up to 5.18 metres have been
reported for animals killed during the nineteenth century.

Longest tooth: The male narwhal has two teeth. The one
on the right normally remains invisible, but the one on the
left grows to a remarkable length. It pierces the animal's
upper lip, develops into a long tusk and eventually looks
rather like a gnarled and twisted walking stick. At least a
third of all narwhal tusks are broken, but unbroken tusks
reach an average length of about two metres. In extreme
cases, they have been known to exceed three metres and
weigh more than 10 kilograms.

Bowhead whale, Nunavut, Arctic Canada

Thickest blubber: The blubber of the bowhead whale is thicker than in any other animal, averaging an incredible 43–50 centimetres. It provides the whale with protection against the freezing cold waters of its Arctic home.

Tallest blow: The 'blow' or 'spout' is the cloud of condensed air and water droplets produced above a whale's head when it blows out. The tallest blow is made by the blue whale: slender and vertical in shape, it can reach an astonishing height of 15 metres – which is clearly visible from several kilometres away.

Fastest: On 12 October 1958, a bull killer whale was timed swimming at 55.5 km/h in the eastern North Pacific. Similar speeds, albeit in short bursts, have also been reported for Dall's porpoises.

Largest appetite: The largest blue whales probably eat as much as 5.5 tonnes of small shrimp-like creatures, called krill, every day. Even an average-sized blue whale is believed to eat about four tonnes. Since each of these tiny animals weighs only about one gramme, a daily intake of about four million of them is required to keep the whale going. In terms of weight, this is equivalent to eating a fully-grown African elephant every day. The whale does not feed year-round, but gorges itself all summer and then fasts during the winter.

Largest prey: Killer whales have been known to prey on more than 25 different whale and dolphin species – and there have been several reported attacks on sperm whales and blues. The largest giant squid known to be taken by a sperm whale was 14.5 metres long, including its tentacles; it was caught on Great Bahama Bank, in the Bahamas.

Noisiest: The low-frequency booms made by blue whales and fin whales when vocalising across enormous stretches of ocean have been measured at up to 188 decibels, making them the loudest sounds emitted by any living source. These remarkable sounds are below the range of human hearing, but with the right equipment they can be detected over distances of up to 3,000 kilometres. It is not yet clear whether they are for long-distance communication or are part of a long-range sonar navigation system for detecting underwater features such as seamounts.

Longest-lived: It is difficult to measure the age of a whale accurately, so the maximum lifespan is not known for most species. However, indirect evidence suggests that some of the larger whales, at least, are able to reach a grand old age of considerably more than 100 years. In 1995, a freshly-killed bowhead whale was being processed in Alaska when the Inuit hunters found two stone harpoon blades embedded in its blubber. Since the use of these particular harpoons ended a century ago, the animal must have been at least 100 years old – and might have survived a lot longer if it had not been killed by people. Meanwhile, scientists have developed a way

Fin whale, New England, USA

CONSERVATION

Endangered species

To the best of our knowledge, no whale, dolphin or porpoise has become extinct in modern times (although no one is certain about the status of the Yangtze river dolphin, or baiji). But a frightening number are in serious trouble, and others have all but disappeared from many of their former haunts.

Considering the magnitude of the problems they face, the odds are firmly stacked against them and, for some at least, the future is undoubtedly bleak.

It is difficult to judge which species is the most endangered. Unfortunately, our knowledge is so inadequate that there are no widely accepted population estimates for the vast majority. Several beaked whales, for example, are known only from stranded specimens and have never been seen alive – but the total lack of observations in the wild does not necessarily mean they are rare, especially since few beaked whales are seen

Some of the rarest whales, dolphins and porpoises in the world

	SPECIES	DISTRIBUTION
1	Yangtze river dolphin or baiji	Yangtze river, China (middle and lower reaches)
2	North Atlantic and North Pacific right whales	North Atlantic and North Pacific
3	Vaquita or Gulf of California porpoise	Extreme northern end of the Gulf of California (Sea of Cortez), Mexico
4	Indus river dolphin	Main channel of the Indus river, Pakistan, downstream of Chashma Barrage
5	Hector's dolphin	Coastal waters of New Zealand (most common around South Island)

regularly. At the same time, the number of survivors is not the only consideration. The blue whale, for example, is not one of the rarest cetaceans in the world but, after decades of intensive whaling, its chances of recovery are severely limited because it is a particularly slow breeder and because its obliterated population is widely dispersed.

The table below summarises five of the rarest whales, dolphins and porpoises for which population figures are known. Of course, it is possible that some poorly-known species are even rarer than the ones on this list.

Yangtze river dolphin, Wuhan, China

POPULATION	NOTES
Likely to be in the low tens or extinct	Now very little chance of rescuing this species, which is likely to become the first cetacean known to become extinct
300 in the North Atlantic; a few hundred in the North Pacific	Hunted almost to extinction by commercial whalers and has never recovered
Fewer than 600	Has the most restricted distribution of any marine cetacean; most commonly seen around the Colorado river delta
Fewer than 1,000	The many threats to its survival include pollution, hunting, fishing and dam construction
Fewer than 3,000	Threatened mainly by entanglement in coastal gillnets (may have reduced population by 50 per cent since 1970)

Whaling

Coastal communities around the world have killed whales for centuries. The blubber and meat provides a welcome source of light, heat and food that is sometimes essential for human survival.

In the old days, this small-scale subsistence hunting probably had only a local impact on whale populations, but by the end of the seventeenth century the character of whaling had changed beyond all recognition. In an age before petroleum or plastics, whales provided valuable raw materials for thousands of everyday products, from soap and candles to whips and corsets. There were huge profits to be made and whaling rapidly became big business.

The slaughter reached its worst excesses around the middle of this century, thanks largely to a series of technological advances in whaling vessels, killing equipment and processing methods. In 1930–31, for example, a record 30,000 blue whales were killed, and in 1963–64, no fewer than 29,255 sperm whales were killed.

Indigenous whaling in the Caribbean

One by one the great whales were hunted almost to the point of extinction. In the space of a few hundred years, literally millions of them were killed around the world. Today, we are left merely with the tattered remains: in most cases, no more than five to 10 per cent of their original populations. There are barely 300 surviving North Atlantic right whales, the bowhead has all but disappeared from vast areas of its former range, and so the catalogue of destruction unfolds. During the twentieth century, more than two million whales were killed in the southern hemisphere alone.

Yet, incredibly, we still have not learnt the lessons of the past. The story of commercial whaling continues as Norway, Iceland and Japan persist in hunting whales in the north Atlantic, the north Pacific and the Antarctic. In blatant defiance of world opinion, they are gradually expanding their activities and, alarmingly, they are being watched with considerable interest by other nations that may ultimately decide to resume whaling themselves.

To make matters even worse, it is virtually impossible to kill whales humanely. In some cases, it can take as long as an hour for them to die agonising deaths after explosive harpoons have blown huge, gaping holes in their bodies. As one ex-whaler commented: 'If whales could scream, whaling would have stopped many years ago'.

Commercial whaling in Iceland

The Faroese pilot whale hunt

Large whales are not the only cetaceans to suffer from hunting. It is believed that tens of thousands of small whales, dolphins and porpoises are killed every year in seas and oceans around the world, although the true extent of the problem is unknown. Nets, knives, rifles, hand-held harpoons and even explosive harpoons are used for the killing.

One of the most controversial of these hunts takes place in the Faroes, a group of islands lying halfway between Scotland and Iceland in the north-east Atlantic. Entire pods of long-finned pilot whales (as well as several dolphin species caught up in the hunt incidentally) are herded into sandy bays by men in small boats, during noisy 'drives' that frequently take many hours to complete. All the animals – including pregnant and lactating females and their babies – are dragged ashore with steel hooks, called gaffs, and then killed with long knives.

Faroese hunting statistics date back to 1584, with unbroken records from 1709 to the present day. During this most recent 295-year period, more than a quarter of a million long-finned pilot whales have been killed in approximately 1,700 different drives. The official number of whales taken each year ranges from zero to a peak of 4,385 recorded in 1941. An average of around 1,200 whales have been taken each year during the past decade.

The Faroese defend the hunt vigorously, arguing that it is a traditional part of their culture and provides a free and welcome source of protein. But opponents of the hunt argue that it is terribly cruel and no longer necessary in such a modern society with a relatively high standard of living; they also argue that no one knows enough about the number of pilot whales around the Faroes, their wider distribution and movements throughout the year, or any of the other dangers they face, to judge whether or not the hunt is a threat to their future survival.

Ironically, recent evidence suggests that it may actually be dangerous to eat long-finned pilot whales taken from the north Atlantic. Their meat and blubber have been found to contain high levels of toxic chemicals and could seriously threaten the health of the Faroese people. At the same time, of course, the presence of so many pollutants inevitably raises concern about the fitness of the whales themselves.

Whale meat drying in the Faroe Islands

Conflicts with fisheries

Since the 1950s, the staggering growth of many modern fisheries and the introduction of increasingly destructive fishing methods have spelt disaster for whales, dolphins and porpoises around the world.

Hundreds of thousands of them – possibly millions – die slow, lingering deaths in fishing nets every year. Many more could be threatened by the sheer scale of modern fisheries, which over-exploit fish stocks with scant regard for the future health of the world's oceans. And in some parts of the world fishermen intentionally kill cetaceans and other marine mammals, either to use as bait or because they view them as competition for 'their' fish. Not surprisingly, few scientists are in any doubt that fishing is the single greatest human-induced cause of mortality in cetaceans.

Drift-netting is one of the worst culprits and, indeed, is probably the most indiscriminate method of fishing ever devised. Hanging in the water, unseen and undetectable, drift nets are carried freely with the ocean currents and winds. Dubbed 'walls of death', or 'curtains of death', they can be hundreds of kilometres long and catch everything in their path from seabirds and turtles to whales and dolphins. In the late 1980s, for instance, the Japanese high-seas squid drift-net fisheries in the north Pacific were killing approximately 15,000–30,000 northern rightwhale dolphins, 11,000 Pacific white-sided dolphins and 6,000 Dall's porpoises every year. The United Nations took action by calling on all member nations to agree to a moratorium on drift-netting by the end of 1992. The global ban has had a very positive impact, but it is being ignored by some Asian countries and whales, dolphins and porpoises continue to be killed in large numbers by drift nets deployed inside the 200 nautical mile limit of many coastal states. More recently, the European Union banned drift-netting in almost all its waters, so progress is being made – albeit too slowly.

Gill nets are similar to drift nets in design, although much smaller, and pose another serious threat. Since they are relatively inexpensive, these death-traps are used along coastlines and in major rivers worldwide, from New Zealand and Sri Lanka to Canada and Britain. Tens of thousands of small cetaceans are believed to drown in them every year.

But perhaps the most infamous culprit, responsible for killing more dolphins in the past 35 years than any other human activity, is the tuna-fishing industry. In the eastern tropical Pacific, a stretch of ocean extending from southern California to Chile and covering an area roughly the size of Canada, it has directly caused the deaths of an estimated six to 12 million dolphins. In the worst period, during the 1960s and early 1970s, as many as half a million dolphins were being killed in the region every year. The eastern spinner dolphin stock was reduced to 44 per cent of its original size in just a few years. Fortunately, public outrage has forced the authorities to introduce new rules and regulations, which include releasing dolphins from the nets when they are captured, and the scale of the slaughter has dropped to thousands (rather than hundreds of thousands) of deaths a year. It is still too many, though, and the effects of stress from capture are an ongoing concern. There is also mounting evidence to suggest that dolphins are being set on by tuna-fishing fleets in other parts of the world.

Unfortunately, there are no easy solutions to most conflicts with fisheries. In some cases, a simple modification of the nets or the fishery management systems can have a positive effect. Educational programmes for fishermen, and newly-developed devices which alert whales and dolphins to the presence of nets, may also work in some situations. But there is no escaping the fact that much more drastic action, such as seasonal closures of some fisheries or dramatic changes in fishing techniques, may be the only effective long-term solution.

Fish on the floor of a fish market, Male, The Maldives

Pollution

Some experts predict that pollution could become the most serious threat to whales, dolphins and porpoises in the future. It is a silent, insidious and widespread killer that is already causing severe problems around the world.

Despite all the warnings, many governments continue to pretend that the world's seas and oceans have an infinite capacity to absorb the waste products of human activities. Ever-increasing quantities of industrial waste, agricultural chemicals, radioactive discharges, untreated sewage, oil, modern plastic debris and a wide variety of other pollutants are dumped directly into the sea every day – or slowly make their way there via rivers – often with devastating effect.

We are only just beginning to learn about the precise details of the damage they cause. Some pollutants are so toxic, or present in such huge quantities, that they cause immediate death. Others are more subtle in their effects, but nonetheless may be responsible for weeks, months or even years of prolonged suffering. They gradually weaken the

Rubbish on beach in Baja California, Mexico

animals, causing hormonal imbalances, a lowering of disease resistance, cancer, and many other abnormalities and chronic health problems; they may even cause a loss of fertility.

Unfortunately, whales, dolphins, porpoises and other top predators are particularly vulnerable to pollution. This is because the toxins are passed along the food chain: minute quantities are picked up by marine plankton, which are then eaten by fish and squid, and these in turn are eaten by the predators themselves. The further along the chain, the higher the concentration of toxins. Worse still, much of this build-up is passed on from one generation to another: a lactating female, through her milk, can deliver the toxins in highly concentrated doses to her young calf.

Habitat degradation, disturbance and noise pollution

One of the greatest threats to wildlife on land is habitat degradation, whether it be tropical rainforest destruction, desertification, wetland drainage or road building across important grasslands and heathland. Whales, dolphins and porpoises also suffer from habitat degradation and disturbance, although in different ways.

The main problem areas are rivers, areas close to the shore, and places near human activities further out to sea. Coastal and riverbank development, land reclamation, deep-sea dumping, oil, gas and mineral exploration, commercial fish farming, boat traffic, and the effects of land-based activities such as deforestation and river damming are all to blame. Their consequences can be quite subtle, such as increased amounts of sediment or changes in salinity, but they can also be extremely dramatic. Habitat degradation along the coast, for example, can have a far-reaching impact on the marine environment as a whole, since this is where nurseries for all kinds of invertebrates and fish form the foundation of the sea's complex food webs.

River dolphins are probably the hardest-hit by habitat degradation. The threats their habitats face include heavy boat traffic, riverbank development and dam construction.

In the case of the highly endangered Yangtze river dolphin, or baiji, for example, the world's largest hydro-electric project at the famous Three Gorges, in Hubei Province, China is likely to be the final nail in its coffin.

To make matters worse, many of the species and populations most affected by habitat degradation already have restricted distributions, or their requirements tie them to coasts or rivers and prevent them from 'escaping' to safer areas. These include all the river dolphins, the vaquita, Burmeister's porpoise, Hector's dolphin, and several large whales that move inshore at certain times of the year to breed.

Even whale watching can be a threat, if it is unregulated. Short-finned pilot whales living off the coast of Tenerife, in the Canary Islands, for example, face a veritable onslaught of whale-watch boats almost every day of the year. Many of the skippers are untrained and unconcerned about their impact on the whales, and their cavalier attitude could affect the long-term survival of the population.

One solution to the problem of habitat degradation and disturbance is to provide the animals with special sanctuaries, or marine reserves, in which they can feed and breed in relative safety. Some already exist, such as around Antarctica and in the Indian Ocean, but they need better legislation to be truly effective. And, of course, many more are needed.

But even marine sanctuaries cannot protect cetaceans from underwater noise pollution. Caused by a variety of human activities, from coastal development and seismic testing to speed boats and heavy shipping, this is a particular problem for whales, dolphins and porpoises which rely on sound for many of their day-to-day activities. Unfortunately, it is not only the loudness of a noise that is important, but its frequency as well – some frequencies are likely to be more disturbing than others, depending on the hearing range of different species. Noise may displace the animals from their feeding or breeding areas and can disrupt critical behaviours such as feeding or caring for young calves. Extremely loud noise can even kill them.

The US Navy's LFAS (Low Frequency Active Sonar) has been in the news a great deal recently – and deservedly so.

Other nations (including the UK) are already operating or planning to operate similar systems within the next few years. LFAS relies on extremely loud, low-frequency sound to detect submarines at great distances and, according to the US Navy's own studies, generates sounds of up to 140 decibels more than 500 kilometres away from the sonar source. During testing off the California coast, the noise was detected on the other side of the North Pacific.

There is growing evidence that this system is extremely harmful to cetaceans – with several mass strandings in different parts of the world coinciding with the testing of military sonar. In September 2002, for example, a mass stranding of three species of beaked whales (totalling 15 animals) occurred during European naval excercises off the Canary Islands. Research has identified a condition in at least some of the animals that resembles decompression sickness (the 'bends'), which occurs in divers who surface too quickly. It is possible that exposure to loud noise caused the whales to ascend faster than their physiology is adapted to allow. The only good news is that, following a legal ruling in 2003, peacetime use of LFAS by the US military has now been significantly limited.

Copacabana Beach, Brazil

In this way, the best operators put something back for the whales. Educational trips help to drum up public support for their cause; the biologists learn more about their lives and needs; there is more money available to tackle important conservation issues; and the local people have good reason to look after the whales and their marine environment.

But ultimately, of course, it is the responsibility of individual whale-watchers to choose the best and most responsible operators before booking a trip.

Clothing and equipment

The ideal choice of clothing and equipment obviously depends on where, when and how you intend to watch whales. But here are a few suggestions:

Suntan lotion and sun hat are essential to avoid sunburn and sunstroke, especially around midday. Because you are more likely to burn at sea than you are on land, use a high factor lotion.

Seasickness tablets or patches should be taken or applied in plenty of time before the trip, if you have any doubts about suffering from seasickness.

Polaroid sunglasses help to reduce the sun's glare and are excellent for seeing through reflections on the surface of the water. Remember to attach them to a safety cord.

Waterproof bags are essential for protecting your spare clothing, binoculars, cameras and other equipment from salty air and spray.

Waterproof jacket and trousers are important if sea conditions are likely to be rough or if you are expecting rain. Spending a day, or even half a day, soaked through to the skin can ruin an entire trip.

Warm and windproof clothing is vital if you are whale watching in cold weather. Remember that it is much colder at sea than it is on shore – so be careful not to underestimate how many layers you are likely to need.

Rubber-soled deck shoes are important in case the deck gets wet with spray. It is easy to slip over if you are wearing inappropriate shoes.

Field notebook and pen are invaluable (some people prefer a pocket-sized dictaphone instead). It's a good idea to copy your notes into a neat version later.

Identification guides are useful for identifying the whales, dolphins or porpoises you encounter. Consider taking guides to the birds, seals, fish and other local wildlife as well.

Binoculars are invaluable for finding whales, dolphins and porpoises, as well as for identifying them and studying their behaviour. Choose image-stabilised binoculars, or a normal pair with a magnification of 7–10x (anything higher will be unusable while you are bouncing around on a boat at sea).

Watching southern right whales, Western Cape, South Africa

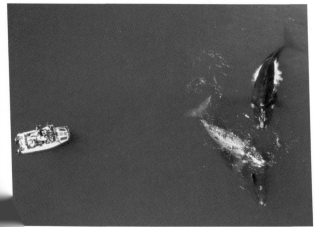

A telescope (with tripod) can be useful when whale-watching from shore, or from the relatively stable platform of a large cruise ship, but the high magnification makes it virtually unusable on smaller boats.

A camera with an 80–200mm lens (or a similar zoom) is ideal but, alternatively, a fixed lens of at least 135mm can be useful for recording close encounters and interesting behaviour patterns. A motordrive is also useful. Do not forget to take plenty of film (at least twice as much as you think you will need) or, if you are using digital, plenty of card space. Use a medium to fast speed (100–200 ISO) depending on the weather and sea conditions.

Hydrophone (underwater microphone). Few whale-watchers carry hydrophones because they are quite expensive and can be difficult to use. But they do help to find some whales by sound, as well as adding a new and exciting dimension to the whale watching experience.

Safety equipment should be provided on all organised whale-watching trips. This might include life jackets, life rafts, flares, a VHF radio, and first aid equipment.

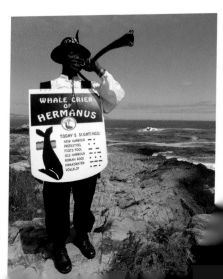

Whale crier,
South Africa

Finding the animals at sea

In theory, it is possible to see whales, dolphins and porpoises almost anywhere in the world. They are found near the poles, at the equator, in freshwater rivers, along shallow coastlines, and even in the deep waters of the open sea.

But many species tend to be plentiful only in particular areas and, even then, are present only at certain times of the year. Their distribution also varies weekly, daily and hourly, according to many different factors such as sea and weather conditions, food availability and human disturbance. To add to the challenge, they can be very difficult to spot in anything but the calmest conditions – even if you are very close to them.

People with a lot of experience at sea instinctively recognise the tiniest clues when they are looking for cetaceans. They are trained to register the slightest movements and splashes that give their presence away. With a large whale, for example, the first clue is often its blow or spout. This is more visible in some weather conditions than others, but it can be surprisingly distinctive. It may look like a flash of white (especially against a dark background) or a more gradual puff of smoke. Blows are easy to miss, though, especially since there is often a considerable gap between each one.

Challenging conditions on the Drake Passage

Alternatively, you may briefly see the head and back of the whale break the surface. This often resembles a strange wave that, somehow, does not look quite right. Anything suspicious, even if nine times out of 10 it does turn out to be a wave, is worth investigating. Splashes are also good clues. They can be caused by a large whale breaching, flipper-slapping or lobtailing – or by dolphins. A group of dolphins in the distance frequently looks like a rough patch of water, resembling lots of whitecaps and little breaking waves. The presence of birds can often be a tell-tale sign as well, particularly if they seem to be feeding or are concentrated in one particular area. It makes sense that, if they have found a school of fish, there could be whales or dolphins feeding underneath.

Finally, do not forget to look *everywhere* – in front, behind, and to both sides. Scan the horizon with binoculars and use the naked eye to check nearer the boat (it is amazing how often people miss dolphins bow-riding right in front of them because they are too busy looking far out to sea). The golden rule is to be patient because, even in areas with well-known cetacean populations, it may take a while to track them down.

Problems of identification

Identifying whales, dolphins and porpoises at sea is a real challenge. In fact, it can be so difficult that even the world's experts are unable to identify every species they encounter: on most official surveys, at least some sightings have to be logged as 'unidentified'. But despite the inevitable frustrations, developing the necessary skills to tell one species from another can also be very satisfying.

There are a number of different problems to overcome. The first, quite simply, is being on a boat: making detailed observations while trying to keep balance on a rolling, slippery deck can be difficult at the best of times. Adverse sea and weather conditions, such as a heavy swell, whitecaps, high winds, driving rain, or even glaring sunshine, add to the difficulties by making it almost impossible to get a good view and an accurate impression of the main features of the animal.

Then there are the whales, dolphins and porpoises themselves. They spend most of their lives underwater and, even when they come to the surface to breathe, frequently reveal little more than a brief glimpse of their dorsal fins and backs. Even a good view can be confusing, since many species look alike: it takes a highly trained eye to tell the difference between a pygmy sperm whale and a dwarf sperm whale, for example.

At the same time, individuals of the same species frequently vary so much that they are rarely identical. Their dorsal fins are shaped differently, they show variations in their colouring, behave differently, and even come in a range of different sizes. Adult bottlenose dolphins, for example, vary in size from just under two metres to nearly four metres.

However, despite all these potential pitfalls, it is quite possible for anyone to recognise the relatively common and distinctive species and, eventually, many of the more unusual ones as well. It just requires some background knowledge and a little practice.

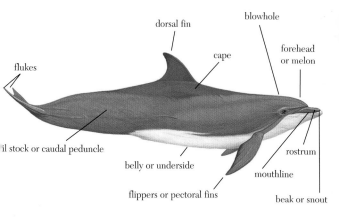

Identification checklist

The easiest way to identify whales, dolphins and porpoises is to use a relatively simple process of elimination. This involves running through a mental checklist of 14 key features every time a new animal is encountered at sea. It is not often possible to use all 14 features, and one alone is rarely enough for a positive identification, but the best approach is to gather information on as many as possible before drawing any firm conclusions.

Geographical location: There is not a single place in the world where all 84 cetacean species have been recorded. In fact, there are not many places with records of more than a few dozen species. This immediately helps to cut down on the number of possibilities. Atlantic white-sided dolphins, for example, occur only in the north Atlantic, while Pacific white-sided dolphins occur only in the north Pacific.

Habitat: Just as cheetahs live on open plains rather than in jungles, and snow leopards prefer mountains to wetlands, most whales, dolphins and porpoises are adapted to specific marine or freshwater habitats. For example, Hector's dolphins are unlikely to be encountered far out to sea, while sperm whales are unlikely to be seen in shallow water.

Killer whale, northern Norway

Size: It is difficult to estimate size accurately at sea, unless a direct comparison can be made with the length of the boat or another object in the water. Therefore it is better to use three simple categories: up to three metres, three to 10 metres, and over 10 metres. In this way, simply by deciding whether the animal is small, medium or large helps to eliminate a wide range of possibilities.

Unusual features: Some cetaceans have very unusual features, which can be used for a quick identification. These include the extraordinary long tusk of the male narwhal and the callosities covering the heads of right whales.

Dorsal fin: The size, shape and position of the dorsal fin varies greatly between species. Some fins are tall and triangular, others are rounded, a few are little more than a hump, some have broad bases, others have narrow bases, some are curved, others are upright, and there is every possible combination in between; and, of course, a few species have no dorsal fin at all. The position of the fin on the animal's back – in the middle, towards the head or towards the tail – is also a useful identification feature.

Flippers: The length, colour and shape of the flippers, as well as their position on the animal's body, vary greatly from

Bryde's whale, Shikoku Island, Japan

Spinner dolphin, The Maldives

one species to another. It is not always possible to see them, but flippers can be useful for identification in some species: in the humpback whale, for example, they are unmistakable.

Body shape: Much of the time, whales, dolphins and porpoises do not show enough of themselves to provide an overall impression of their shape. Sometimes, however, this can be a useful feature. For example, the vaquita has a noticeably robust body shape, while the finless porpoise is quite slender and streamlined.

Beak: The presence or absence of a prominent beak is a particularly useful identification feature in toothed whales. The Irrawaddy dolphin, for instance, has a rounded head without an obvious beak, whereas the spinner dolphin has a very long, narrow beak.

Colour and markings: Many cetaceans are surprisingly colourful, and have distinctive markings such as body stripes or eye patches. Commerson's dolphins, for example, are markedly black and white, while Risso's dolphins are usually covered in white scratches and scars. Unfortunately, more subtle markings can be difficult to use for identification purposes, because colours at sea vary according to water clarity and light conditions. Also, bear in mind that the animal can appear much darker than normal if it is viewed against the sun.

Flukes: The flukes can be important features for identifying larger whales: some species lift their flukes high into the air before they dive, others do not. Minke and sei whales generally do not, for example, while humpbacks and sperm whales frequently do. It is also worth checking the shape of the flukes, looking for any distinctive markings and noticing whether or not there is a notch between the trailing edges.

Blow or spout: The blow is only really visible in larger whales. But it varies in height, shape and visibility between species and, especially on calm days, can be extremely useful for identification purposes. Although variations in the blow between individuals can make it a tricky means of identification, experienced observers can tell one species from another even from a considerable distance. Right whales, for example, have wide, V-shaped blows, whereas fin whales produce single, narrow columns of spray.

Dive sequence: The dive sequence can be surprisingly distinctive in many species. Variations include: the angle at which the head breaks the surface; whether or not the dorsal fin and blowhole are visible at the same time; how strongly the tail stock is arched; the time interval between breaths; and the number of breaths before a deep dive.

Behaviour: Some species are more active at the surface than others, so any unusual behaviour can sometimes be useful for identification purposes. Among the large whales, for instance, humpbacks and right whales breach much more often than fin whales and blue whales.

Group size: Since some species are highly gregarious, while others tend to live alone or in small groups, it is worth noting the number of animals seen together. Fin whales, for example, are normally seen alone or in small groups, whereas there could be dozens or hundreds of long-finned pilot whales travelling together, or literally thousands of common dolphins.

Short-finned pilot whales, Sea of Cortez, Mexico

The golden rule

It is often tempting to guess the identification of an unusual whale, dolphin or porpoise that you have not seen very clearly. But this is a mistake. Apart from the fact that it is bad science, it does little to improve your identification skills. Working hard at identification – and then enjoying the satisfaction of knowing that an animal has been identified correctly – is what makes a real expert in the long term.

It is perfectly acceptable to record simply 'unidentified dolphin' or 'unidentified whale', if a more accurate identification is not possible. But do write detailed notes for reference at a later date. As well as helping to improve your field skills, these notes may enable repeat sightings of species previously recorded as 'unidentified' to be turned into a positive identification days, weeks, months or even years later.

Recognising behaviour patterns

Whales, dolphins and porpoises are active animals and some of their more impressive and energetic displays take place in full view on the surface of the water. They slap the water with their flippers, fins or tails, ride in the bow waves and wakes of boats, lift their heads above the surface, and even leap high into the air and land back in the water with a tremendous splash.

Grey whale, San Ignacio Lagoon, Mexico

We do not fully understand the meaning of many of these displays and, of course, it is quite possible that there are different explanations for different occasions, according to the species, the age and sex of the animal, and the context in which the activities are taking place.

However, a great deal of behavioural research has been done in recent years and, at last, we are beginning to unravel some of their secrets. Slapping the surface, for example, may be a form of courtship display, a way of signalling across great distances underwater, a technique for herding fish or dislodging parasites, a show of strength or a challenge... or, in some cases, it could simply be for fun.

Breaching: When a whale launches itself into the air head-first, and falls back into the water with a splash, it is said to be breaching. Most species have been observed breaching at one time or another, although some do it more often than others. Tail breaching is similar, but is tail-first instead of head-first and rarely lifts the whale as far out of the water.

Flipper-slapping: Many cetaceans lie on their sides or backs and slap one or both of their flippers onto the surface with a resounding splash. This is known as flipper-slapping, pectoral-slapping, pec-slapping or flipper-flopping.

Lobtailing: Lobtailing is an impressive display, especially in large whales, involving the forceful slapping of the flukes against the surface of the water. Also known as tail-slapping, it is done while the main body of the whale lies just under the surface.

Southern right whale, Western Cape, South Africa

Blowing or spouting: The blow or spout is the cloud of condensed air and atomised water droplets (not water) produced above a whale's head when it breathes out. It is also the term used to describe the actual act of breathing. In most small whales, dolphins and porpoises, the blow is low, brief and barely visible, but in large whales it can be very distinctive.

Fluking: When some large whales make a deep dive from the surface, they lift their tails high into the air to thrust their bodies into a more steeply-angled descent toward deeper waters. Bowheads, right whales, greys, blues, humpbacks and sperm whales all lift their flukes regularly, while a number of other species do from time to time. All whales leave a 'flukeprint' at the surface – a circular swirl looking like a patch of oil – made by turbulence from the movement of the flukes.

Spyhopping: Spyhopping is the term used to describe an interesting form of behaviour in which whales and dolphins poke their heads above the surface of the water, apparently to have a look around. Most species can see both above and below the surface.

Wake-riding: Swimming in the frothy wake of a boat or ship seems to be a favourite pastime of many dolphins, as well as some whales and porpoises. They surf, twist and turn in the waves, and even splash around and swim upside-down in the bubbles.

Logging: It is not uncommon to see groups of whales floating motionless at the surface together, usually all facing in the same direction. Known as logging, this is a form of rest.

Porpoising: When travelling at speed, many cetaceans literally leave the water each time they take a breath. Also known as running, this is believed to reduce friction on their bodies when they break the surface, which may help to conserve energy.

Bow-riding: Many dolphins, and some whales and porpoises, ride the bow-waves of boats and ships, jostling for the best position where they can be pushed along in the water by the force of the wave. Certain dolphins even ride the bow-waves of large whales in exactly the same way. On some occasions they may simply be hitching a free ride but, when they actively go out of their way to ride in the bow-waves, it is difficult to imagine that it can be anything more than exuberant play.

Bow-riding Heaviside's dolphins, Western Cape, South Africa

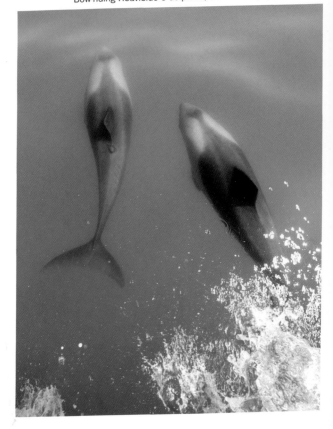

HOW WHALES AND DOLPHINS ARE STUDIED

Research on wild whales is staggeringly new. It is so new, in fact, that whale biologists have yet to monitor a single generation of large whales through one complete life cycle, from the moment they are born to their last days and ultimately to death through old age.

For years, the prospect of studying whales must have seemed about as difficult and challenging as exploring outer space. After all, these are animals that often live in extremely remote areas far out to sea, spend much of their lives diving to great depths underwater, and then show little of themselves when they rise to the surface to breathe. Many are quite shy and elusive, as well, and tend to avoid boats so, even at the surface, close encounters with them are almost impossible.

From early beginnings to high-tech research

For a long time, the only information we had came from dead animals washed ashore, or killed by fishermen, and from some of the millions of whales slaughtered by commercial whalers. Then scientists began to study captive bottlenose dolphins and other small cetaceans in their concrete tanks.

But as we accumulated a wealth of data on basic whale biology, our knowledge of their lives under natural conditions, wild and free, was severely limited. In the days when modern technology had already taken us to the Moon and beyond, we were only just beginning to understand these extraordinary forms of intelligent life on our own planet. As one biologist commented, 'the best we can say is that our knowledge of whales, dolphins and porpoises has progressed from almost nothing to just a little bit'.

The first attempts at wild whale research concentrated simply on counting whales – dead ones, initially, because they were so much easier to count than live ones. It was not until the late 1960s and early 1970s that a few pioneer biologists began the painstaking process of counting live whales, and then trying to learn more about their feeding techniques, breeding habits, migrations and other aspects of their daily lives.

Gradually, more and more people became involved in whale research, and their information-gathering techniques became increasingly sophisticated. In the past decade, the number of researchers, projects and study locations has increased exponentially, while whale research itself has become a leading branch of natural science.

Modern whale researchers still study whales in the traditional sense, simply watching them through binoculars, for example, or leaning out of boats to scoop up their faeces for examination. But, at the same time, they frequently enlist the help of state-of-the-art equipment and the kind of enterprising and visionary research techniques that would make NASA proud.

Satellites in space, deep-sea submersibles, radio transmitters, high-tech directional hydrophones, complex computer programmes, fibre optics, deepwater video

Bottlenose dolphin, Sea of Cortez, Mexico

probes, DNA fingerprinting and, most recently, the US Navy's Integrated Underwater Surveillance System are now all part of the modern whale researcher's armoury.

Photo-identification

Biologists have been identifying individual animals as part of their research for a long time. It is an invaluable way of following their movements, activities and associations over periods of days, weeks, months and even years. Jane Goodall used facial patterns to recognise all the chimpanzees in her classic study in Gombe National Park, Tanzania, for example; more recent studies have used striping patterns in zebras, the arrangement of whiskers in lions, and even the shapes, nicks and scars of elephants' ears to tell one animal from another.

Whale and dolphin biologists are no exception, and they identify individuals in many different ways. Blue whales can be recognised by the shape of the dorsal fin and the pattern of mottling on the body; individual humpback whales, on the other hand, are recognised by the unique black-and-white markings on the underside of the tail. The differences can often be quite subtle, so each animal is photographed to confirm its identity and to provide a permanent record of its existence. This technique is known as 'photo-identification', or 'photo-ID', and has dramatically extended our knowledge of wild cetaceans in recent years.

DNA fingerprinting

Do different calves with the same mother share the same father? Are individuals that spend a lot of time together related? These and many other intriguing questions can be answered just by examining a small piece of a whale's skin. More accurately, it is the genetic material, or DNA, in the skin that is so revealing. Just as one person's fingerprints are different from everyone else's, no two animals have exactly the same DNA – yet related animals show some similarities. The clever detective work involved in interpreting this information is called 'DNA fingerprinting', and it has proved invaluable in wild whale research.

Radio- and satellite-telemetry

It is possible to attach a specially
designed transmitter to a whale or
dolphin and then follow its
movements from a boat, a light
aircraft or even a research
laboratory on the other side
of the world. Some
transmitters are merely
tracking devices, but
more sophisticated
models can also
provide
information on
the animal's swimming patterns, dive depths and heart rate,
as well as environmental conditions, water temperature, and
much more. There are basically two kinds of transmitter:
radio transmitters, which send signals directly to receivers
nearby, and satellite transmitters, which beam the signals up
to orbiting communications satellites and from there back to
receiving stations anywhere on Earth.

Eavesdropping on the underwater world

Whales, dolphins and porpoises live in a world that is
dominated by sound, and a great deal can be learnt by listening
to them underwater. This is such a challenging area of research
that it has been likened to trying to find out what goes on in
New York by dangling a microphone from the top of the
Empire State Building. But experienced whale scientists using
sophisticated underwater microphones, called hydrophones,
have been making some exciting discoveries in recent years.

A major development in this field came in 1992, when the
US Navy opened its doors to the so-called Integrated
Underwater Surveillance System. A series of sophisticated
underwater listening stations on the seabed, originally designed
for tracking enemy submarines, this offers some tremendously
exciting possibilities for whale research in the future.

The whale jigsaw

There are still no short-cuts in whale research but, in recent years, the growth in our knowledge has been nothing short of remarkable. Studying such elusive creatures is all about being content with tiny snippets of information that must be assembled into a coherent picture over periods of many years. It is like piecing together an enormously complicated jigsaw puzzle, where each piece brings with it new questions and unexpected surprises. The main difference, of course, is that the whale jigsaw will never be completely finished. Nevertheless, it is encouraging to know that we have probably added more pieces in the past 10 or 20 years than ever before.

Sperm whales,
Sea of Cortez,
Mexico

Grey Whale
Eschrichtius robustus

ID FACT FILE

OTHER NAMES
California grey whale, mussel-digger, devilfish, scrag whale.

MAXIMUM LENGTH
15 metres.

MAXIMUM WEIGHT
35 tonnes.

FIELD ID
Mottled grey; low hump instead of fin; 'knuckles' between hump and tail; low heart-shaped blow; narrow head with barnacles and whale lice; usually raises flukes when diving.

DIET
Mainly benthic amphipods, filtered from bottom sediment; also midwater fish and crustaceans.

BREEDING
Calves every 2–3 years; gestation 12–13 months.

By the time the grey whale was being given official protection, in the late 1930s, it was already extinct in the North Atlantic and was dangerously close to extinction in the North Pacific. It is unclear why the North Atlantic population had disappeared a few hundred years earlier, but whaling in the North Pacific was so intense that it left no more than a few hundred survivors. Fortunately, there were just enough for the grey whale to make a remarkable comeback – so remarkable, in fact, that its recovery is unmatched by any other species of great whale. The current population of some 26,000 Californian grey whales may even exceed pre-exploitation levels. However, the population in the western North Pacific is still critically endangered, with as few as 100 animals remaining. Once dubbed the devilfish by whalers, for their ferocity in the face of danger, grey whales are better known these days for their friendly behaviour and curious approaches to boats.

Where to look

Grey whales are found only in the North Pacific. The eastern population (Californian stock) migrates on average about 8,000 kilometres

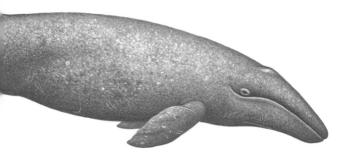

between its summer feeding grounds in the
Arctic's Bering, Chukchi and western Beaufort
seas and its winter breeding grounds around Baja
California, Mexico. The western population
(Korean stock) spends the summer in the Sea of
Okhotsk and is believed to breed in tropical waters
off southern China.

INCREDIBLE JOURNEYS OF THE GREY WHALE

Grey whales are inveterate travellers, commuting along the entire length of the North American coastline, and back again, every year. The round-trip distance between their winter breeding grounds in Baja California, Mexico, and their summer feeding grounds in the Bering Sea can be as much as 20,000 kilometres, making their journey one of the longest migrations of any mammal. The migration north tends to be close to shore and in good weather, the one south often takes place in stormier weather and is usually a little further offshore (although still within sight of land).

Feeding in the Arctic: April–October

The vast majority of grey whales spend every summer in the Bering, Chukchi and western Beaufort seas where, for about five months of the year, they eat as much as they possibly can. Feeding in relatively shallow water, they use their mouths like vacuum cleaners and literally suck up sediment from the seabed. They sieve this with their baleen plates, and then swallow the tiny crustaceans trapped inside. Each adult grey whale eats nearly 70 tonnes of these little creatures in one summer-long feast. Their aim is to put on enough body weight, in the form of blubber and fat, to survive the rest of the year without food.

Migrating south: November–February

Early in October, the Arctic weather begins to worsen and the whales prepare themselves to leave. Their migration south is organised like a military manoeuvre: the pregnant females are first to go, followed by non-pregnant females, then mature males, immature females next and, finally, the immature males. Over a period of several months, they file through Unimak Pass, a narrow gap between islands in the Aleutian chain, and head south. By the second week of January, huge numbers are passing southern California. With hardly a break, they average about 125 kilometres a day, and the entire journey takes them a couple of months.

GREY WHALE

Breeding in the sub-tropics: December–April

The pregnant females are the first to arrive in the breeding lagoons along the Pacific coast of Baja California, Mexico. They give birth to their calves, in the shallow backwaters, while many of the other whales are still on their way south. The calves drink huge quantities of their mothers' fat-laden milk and gain weight rapidly. It is a race against time, because within a few months they will have to be fit and ready for their first journey north.

Migrating north: February–June

The grey whales tend to swim a little slower on their journey north (perhaps 70–90 kilometres a day) and the females with calves, especially, rest for a few hours or even a few days at a time. Funnelling back into the Bering Sea, through Unimak Pass, they fan out across their Arctic feeding grounds for another summer. It will only be a few months before they are ready to leave once again and, as one yearly cycle comes to an end, another begins.

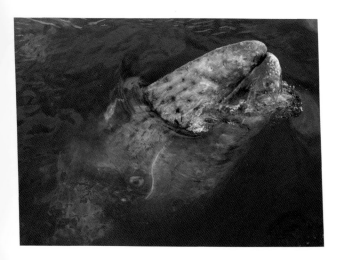

Southern Right Whale
Eubalaena australis

ID FACT FILE

OTHER NAMES
Black right whale.

MAXIMUM LENGTH
17 metres.

MAXIMUM WEIGHT
90 tonnes.

FIELD ID
Black with irregular white patches on underside; broad back with no fin; large head covered in callosities; strongly arched mouthline; large paddle-shaped flippers; V-shaped blow; usually raises flukes when diving.

DIET
Mainly copepods (which are so small about 8,000 would fit in a teaspoon); occasionally krill.

BREEDING
Calves every 3–5 years; gestation 12 months.

With their enormous heads covered in strange-looking callosities (hardened patches of skin), their dark, rotund bodies, and their lack of a dorsal fin, northern and southern right whales look almost identical. But they have long been considered distinct species and this separation has recently been supported by genetic evidence. Southern right whales have been studied since 1970 – longer than any other baleen whale – when Roger Payne began to recognise individuals by the shape and pattern of their callosities at Peninsula Valdés, Argentina. Right whales are particularly active at the surface and can often be seen breaching, lobtailing, spyhopping and even sailing (they raise flukes in the air and then sail downwind before swimming back to the starting point for another go). Their mating system is unusual among whales because it is heavily dependent on sperm competition (male right whales have the largest testes in the animal kingdom – weighing nearly a tonne) rather than competition between individuals.

Where to look

The southern right whale has a circumpolar distribution in the southern hemisphere. It breeds in South America, southern Africa and Australasia (and off several remote offshore islands such as Crozet and Kerguelen). Its summer feeding grounds are in colder waters around Antarctica and elsewhere in the Southern Ocean. Exploited heavily during the nineteenth century, its numbers now appear to be recovering well.

Northern Right Whale

Eubalaena glacialis (North Atlantic)
Eubalaena japonica (North Pacific)

ID FACT FILE

OTHER NAMES
Black right whale, Biscayan right whale, Nordkaper.
MAXIMUM LENGTH
18 metres.
MAXIMUM WEIGHT
100 tonnes.
FIELD ID
Black with irregular white patches on underside; broad back with no fin; large head covered in callosities; strongly arched mouthline; large paddle-shaped flippers; V-shaped blow; usually raises flukes when diving.
DIET
Mainly copepods (which are so small about 8,000 would fit in a teaspoon); occasionally krill.
BREEDING
Calves every 3–5 years; gestation 12 months.

Recent genetic evidence suggests that there are two species of northern right whale, and that they have been evolving separately for millennia. However, they look virtually identical with their raised and roughened patches of skin, known as callosities. These occur on the whales in approximately the same places as facial hair on human males and, although they are black, usually appear white or orangey-white due to massive infestations of whale lice. Callosities are found on both sexes and young calves, but their purpose is unknown. Northern right whales are the rarest large whales in the world and have never recovered from years of heavy exploitation by whalers. There are only about 300 North Atlantic right whales surviving today. Estimates for North Pacific right whales are less precise, but there are probably fewer than 100 left in the eastern population (just one calf has been seen here in the past century) and possibly a few hundred in the western population.

Where to look

The largest population is in the western North Atlantic – mainly off Cape Cod in spring, the Bay of Fundy and the Scotia Shelf in summer, and on breeding grounds off Florida and Georgia in winter. There are very occasional sightings in European waters. Small numbers survive in the North Pacific, mainly from the Sea of Okhotsk east to the Gulf of Alaska, with occasional sightings off the United States and Baja California, Mexico.

NORTHERN RIGHT WHALES: ON THE VERGE OF EXTINCTION

North Atlantic right whales were probably the first whales to be hunted commercially: Basque whalers were killing them in the Bay of Biscay, north of Spain, as early as the eleventh century. The whales were killed primarily for their oil, which was distributed throughout Europe, but the Basques found a market for almost every part of their catch and even the excrement was used (for dyeing fabrics red). The whaling had spread to eastern Canada by 1530 and to New England by the 1600s and right whales continued to be popular targets for commercial whalers for many centuries. Whaling of North Pacific right whales began considerably later, in the Gulf of Alaska in 1835, but was no less intensive.

Named for being the 'right' whales to catch, they were easy to approach, slow swimmers, lived close to shore, normally floated when dead, and provided large quantities of valuable oil, meat and baleen (whalebone). By the early 1900s, tens or even hundreds of thousands of them had been killed, and all three species were critically close to extinction.

All right whale populations worldwide were protected from commercial whaling in the late 1930s, although some were killed illegally by Japan, Brazil and the Soviet Union well into the 1950s and 1960s. But even after decades of international legal protection, only the southern right whale is showing signs of recovery.

Although the whaling has ceased, North Atlantic right whales are now threatened by heavy shipping and entanglement in commercial fishing gear. Between 1970 and 1999, no fewer than 16 were known to have been killed in collisions with ships (and two others probably died of their injuries), while three are known to have drowned in fishing nets and a further eight were seriously injured and probably died too. When the surviving population is so small, these are significant numbers. The sad fact is that northern right whales are among the world's most critically endangered mammals and are probably closer to extinction than any other large whale.

Pygmy Right Whale
Caperea marginata

ID FACT FILE

OTHER NAMES
None.

MAXIMUM LENGTH
6.5 metres.

MAXIMUM WEIGHT
3.4 tonnes.

FIELD ID
Quite small and sleek; grey upperside, paler underside; pronounced falcate fin; may be twin chevrons on back and sides; strongly arched mouth-line; no callosities on head; indistinct blow; undemonstrative behaviour; rarely raises flukes when diving.

DIET
Probably copepods, but also some krill.

BREEDING
Calving interval and gestation period unknown.

The pygmy right whale is the smallest species of baleen whale and one of the least-known cetaceans. Our knowledge is based on fewer than 20 sightings at sea and a few dozen dead animals caught by fishermen or washed ashore. Like the other right whales it has a strongly arched lower jaw, but it differs from them in having a pronounced dorsal fin and no callosities. It is the only baleen whale that has not been the target of large-scale commercial whaling and the only known threat is occasional drownings in fishing nets off South Africa. Pygmy right whales are usually seen alone or in pairs, although large aggregations of as many as 80 individuals have been recorded. Virtually nothing is known about their social structure or behaviour. Unless it is possible to see the distinctive arched mouthline, they can be very difficult to distinguish from dwarf and Antarctic minke whales at sea.

Where to look

The pygmy right whale is known from a small number of widely dispersed records across temperate waters of the southern hemisphere (never south of the Antarctic Convergence). It has been recorded mainly in Australasia, South Africa, South America and a few islands in between.

Bowhead Whale

Balaena mysticetus

ID FACT FILE

OTHER NAMES
Greenland right whale, Greenland whale, Arctic right whale, Arctic whale.

MAXIMUM LENGTH
20 metres.

MAXIMUM WEIGHT
90 tonnes.

FIELD ID
Black, rotund body; no fin; irregular white patch on chin with black spots; two distinct humps in profile; huge head; strongly arched mouth; V-shaped blow; no callosities or barnacles; often raises flukes when diving.

DIET
Mainly krill and copepods, but also other invertebrates.

BREEDING
Calves every 3–4 years; gestation probably 13–14 months.

The only large whale found exclusively in the Arctic, the bowhead is well adapted to life in its freezing home. With a layer of blubber up to 50 centimetres thick, and an ability to create its own breathing holes by breaking through ice up to 1.8 metres thick, it is able to live in higher latitudes than any other baleen whale. Its distinctive head is almost triangular in profile and, when lying at the surface, forms the first of two humps (the second is the back) that make it resemble the shape of the Loch Ness Monster. There is growing evidence that, like humpback whales, bowhead males produce songs that may advertise for females. Heavily hunted by commercial whalers for several centuries, and still being taken by small-scale indigenous whalers, the bowhead is not particularly common. The total number of survivors is estimated to be only 8,000–9,000, and most of these live in a single population in the Bering, Chukchi and Beaufort Seas. The remaining four recognised populations are highly endangered.

Where to look
Bowhead whales are found in cold waters around the Arctic and sub-Arctic, rarely far from the pack ice. They normally migrate to the high Arctic in spring and summer, as the sea ice breaks up and recedes, and then retreat southwards with the advancing ice edge in autumn and winter.

Humpback Whale
Megaptera novaeangliae

ID FACT FILE

OTHER NAMES
Hump-backed whale.
MAXIMUM LENGTH
17 metres.
MAXIMUM WEIGHT
40 tonnes.
FIELD ID
Stocky body; black upperside, white, black or mottled underside; low, stubby fin often on a hump; extremely long flippers white below and white or black (North Pacific) above; single, bushy blow; variable black-and-white fluke pattern; often raises flukes when diving.

DIET
Krill and variety of small schooling fish.
BREEDING
Calves every 2–3 years; gestation about 12 months.

The humpback whale is relatively well studied, yet many aspects of its life are still shrouded in mystery and we are only just beginning to unravel some of its best-kept secrets. It is renowned for its long flippers, which can grow to nearly a third of its body length and give the humpback its scientific name (*Megaptera novaeangliae* means 'big-winged New Englander' – New England being where the first specimen was described). Its head is also distinctive, with a series of knobs or tubercles covering the rostrum and much of the lower jaw; about the size of a golf ball, each knob is a hair follicle with a single, coarse hair growing out of its centre. Humpbacks are among the most energetic of all the large whales and are well known for their spectacular breaching, as well as lobtailing, flipper-

HUMPBACK WHALE

slapping and spyhopping. Even when they seem to be resting, they are fun to watch and may lie on their backs, or sides, holding their enormous flippers high in the air.

Where to look
Widely distributed from the poles to the tropics, humpbacks feed in cool waters during spring and summer and breed in warmer water during the winter. They migrate farther than most other cetaceans – making a round-trip journey of up to 16,000 kilometres. Nearly a quarter of a million were killed by commercial whalers, but they seem to be making a good recovery in many parts of their range.

FISHING WITH NETS OF BUBBLES

Humpback whales have developed an extraordinarily diverse and ingenious range of techniques for catching their food. They lunge through patches of fish or krill with their mouths wide open, literally gulping vast mouthfuls out of the ocean, and even stun their prey with slaps of their flippers or flukes.

But no fishing technique is more impressive than fishing with bubbles. Many humpbacks use huge, explosive bubble clouds, releasing a single blast up to 20 metres across that probably concentrates and disorientates their prey. But to catch herring in the northern North Pacific and Bering Sea they prefer more delicate bubble nets, which strongly resemble man-made seine nets both in design and in the way they are deployed.

Known simply as 'bubble-netting', this particular fishing technique is all the more sensational because the climax of the action takes place in full view above the surface of the water.

When a humpback whale forms a bubble net on its own, it dives beneath a school of fish and starts to release bubbles from its blowholes. Then it swims slowly towards the surface, in a spiral, to form a circular barrier of bubbles around the school. As soon as the 'net' is complete, it swims through the centre with its mouth wide open. The water is flushed out through the baleen plates, as the whale rises above the surface, and the fish trapped inside its mouth are swept up by the tongue and swallowed.

Incredibly, as many as 20 humpback whales may work together in a more complex form of bubble-net fishing, requiring an almost incomprehensible level of coordination.

It begins with all the members of a fishing group swimming slowly at the surface, spending a few minutes resting and catching their collective breath. Then they all dive and disappear beneath the surface together. No one knows quite how they organise themselves underwater but, after about five or 10 minutes, bubbles begin to break the surface, each one roughly the size of a dinner plate. These form part of a huge circle that can be up to 45 metres across. Suddenly, hundreds of tonnes of blubber and gaping mouths erupt from within the circle in one great foaming mass. With water gushing down their distended throat pleats, and fish leaping for their lives, the whales explode to a height of nearly six metres before sinking back into the depths. It is one of the greatest wildlife spectacles on Earth.

Opposite: Lunge-feeding humpback whale, south-east Alaska

SINGING HUMPBACKS

Drop a hydrophone into the water in an area where
humpback whales are breeding and you may hear a baffling
medley of moans, groans, roars, snores, squeaks and
whistles. These are the unearthly, hauntingly beautiful
sounds made by male humpback whales, which are famous
for singing the longest and most complex songs in the
animal kingdom.

The singing whales hang almost upside-down in the
water, often fairly close to the surface. With their eyes
closed and their heads pointing towards the seabed, they
sometimes wave their enormous flippers up and down like
conductors in front of an orchestra.

Humpback whale, Silver Bank, Dominican Republic

No one knows exactly how they sing. They have no vocal chords and, intriguingly, while they are in full song, no air is released. They do not even open their mouths. The latest theory is that they shift air around inside their bodies, but much more research is needed before it is possible to be sure of the details.

They sing throughout the day and night – and may continue for 24 hours or even longer with hardly a break. Because most of the singing takes place at the breeding grounds, and exclusively by males, it is probably used to woo females and to warn away unwanted competition from rival males. But it is also possible that the songs have more subtle meanings and nuances that we do not yet understand.

A song can last for as long as half an hour and, as soon as the whale has finished, it simply goes back to the beginning and sings the same song all over again. Each song consists of several main components, or phrases, which are always sung in the same order and are repeated a number of times but are forever being refined and improved. This means that the song heard one day is quite different to the one being heard several months later. When the whales return to their breeding grounds the following winter, they immediately start singing the version of the song that was in vogue at the end of the previous breeding season.

Even more extraordinary is the fact that all the humpbacks in one area sing broadly the same song, incorporating each other's improvisations as they go along. It is as if they compose and then re-write the 'music' together. In this way, the entire composition changes over a period of several years.

Meanwhile, humpback whales in other oceans sing very different compositions. They probably all croon about the same trials and tribulations in life, but it is as if the ones living around Hawaii sing in American English, while those living off the coast of the Dominican Republic, for example, sing in Caribbean English. The differences are so distinctive that experts can tell where a whale was recorded simply by listening to the intricacies of its own special dialect.

Common Minke Whale

Balaenoptera acutorostrata

ID FACT FILE

OTHER NAMES
Little finner, little piked whale, pikehead, lesser finback, lesser rorqual.

MAXIMUM LENGTH
10.7 metres.

MAXIMUM WEIGHT
9 tonnes.

FIELD ID
Small and sleek; dark upperside, white underside; sharply-pointed snout; snout breaks surface first; falcate fin; white bands on flippers in many populations; indistinct or invisible blow; does not raise flukes when diving.

DIET
Mainly small schooling fish and krill.

BREEDING
Calves every 1–2 years; gestation about 10 months.

The common minke is the second smallest baleen whale, after the pygmy right, and is also the commonest. Reputedly named after a novice eighteenth-century Norwegian whaler, named Meincke, it is a frequent sight on whale-watch trips in many parts of the world. Surprisingly little is known about many aspects of its life, though, and limited evidence suggests an intriguingly complex social structure with populations segregated by age, sex or reproductive condition. Minkes are quite variable in appearance: animals in the northern hemisphere, for example, have a white band on their flippers, but this extends into a white shoulder patch or is absent on many southern hemisphere animals. Two sub-species are recognised – North Atlantic minke whale (*Balaenoptera acutorostrata acutorostrata*) and North Pacific minke whale (*Balaenoptera acutorostrata scammoni*) – and there may be a third, known as the dwarf minke whale for its smaller size, found only in the southern hemisphere. Minkes are curious and will approach boats.

Where to look

Found virtually worldwide from the tropics to the edge of the polar ice, mainly in warmer waters in winter and cooler waters in summer. The minke whale's small size saved it from commercial whalers until the twentieth century, but many tens of thousands have been killed in the last hundred years. It is still being hunted today, by Norway and Iceland in the North Atlantic and Japan in the North Pacific and the Antarctic.

Antarctic Minke Whale

Balaenoptera bonaerensis

ID FACT FILE

OTHER NAMES
Little finner, little piked whale, pikehead, lesser finback, lesser rorqual.

MAXIMUM LENGTH
10.7 metres.

MAXIMUM WEIGHT
9 tonnes.

FIELD ID
Small and sleek; dark upperside, white underside; asymmetrical baleen colouration; sharply-pointed snout; snout breaks surface first; falcate fin; flippers may be light-coloured but no white bands; indistinct or invisible blow; does not raise flukes when diving.

DIET
Mainly krill, but sometimes small schooling fish.

BREEDING
Calves every 1–2 years; gestation about 10 months.

A new species of minke whale, the Antarctic minke, was officially recognised in the late 1990s. It differs significantly from the common minke in many external and skeletal features (its baleen plates, for example, have an asymmetrical colouration) and the two species are so genetically different that they are more closely related to sei and Bryde's whales than they are to each other. However, they can be difficult to tell apart at sea. Antarctic minkes overlap in range with dwarf minkes (a smaller form of the common minke) but on average are a full two metres longer. They are usually seen alone or in small groups, although larger gatherings are sometimes encountered on good feeding grounds. They are believed to form a significant part of the diet of Antarctic killer whales and are still being killed by Japan for the dubious purpose of scientific research. In the past century, whalers have killed more than 100,000 minke whales in the southern hemisphere and most of these were probably Antarctic minkes.

Where to look

As its name suggests, the Antarctic minke whale spends summer in the cold waters around Antarctica – from about 55°S through the deep waters of the Southern Ocean and right up to the ice edge. Little is known about its seasonal migrations, but most individuals probably spend the winter between about 7°S and 35°S. A few may reach as far north as the equator.

Antarctic minke whales, Antarctic Peninsula

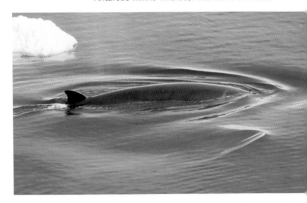

Bryde's Whale
Balaenoptera edeni

ID FACT FILE

OTHER NAMES
Tropical whale.
MAXIMUM LENGTH
15.5 metres.
MAXIMUM WEIGHT
40 tonnes.
FIELD ID
Dark, smoky grey
upperside, white
underside
(upperside may
appear brown in
some lights);
skin may be
mottled; three
parallel
longitudinal
ridges on head;
prominent,
falcate fin;
narrow, hazy
blow; arches
back but does
not raise flukes
when diving.
DIET
Mainly small
schooling fish,
but also krill.
BREEDING
Calves every 2
years; gestation
about 12
months.

Bryde's whale is named after a
Norwegian called Johan Bryde, who was
a whaling pioneer in South Africa. The
least-known of the large baleen whales, it
is unusual because it does not seem to
migrate long distances between separate
feeding and breeding grounds every year.
It stays in warm waters, and may even eat
and breed in the same general area. In
the past Bryde's whales that were caught
by whalers were often mistakenly
recorded as sei whales, but they are
unique in having three longitudinal
ridges along the top of the head (all other
members of the family have just one).
The history of whaling for Bryde's whales
is largely unknown, because of the
confusion with sei whales, but in recent
years Japanese whalers have been taking
this species in the North Pacific. There
may be more than one species and,
indeed, it is likely that a pygmy form of
Bryde's whale will be assigned separate
species status in the near future.

Where to look

Bryde's whales are found in tropical to temperate
waters worldwide. Rarely moving farther north or
south than 40°, they occur both offshore and near
the coast. There seem to be specific pockets of
abundance where there is unusually high
productivity, such as off southern Africa and western
Australia. The pygmy form is known from the
eastern Indian Ocean, the western Pacific and
Australasia and may yet be found elsewhere.

Sei Whale

Balaenoptera borealis

ID FACT FILE

OTHER NAMES
Sardine whale,
pollack whale,
coalfish whale,
Rudolphi's
rorqual, finner.
MAXIMUM LENGTH
19 metres.
MAXIMUM WEIGHT
45 tonnes.
FIELD ID
Large, sleek
body; dark grey
upperside, white
or creamy
underside; often
has oval-shaped
scars; single
longitudinal ridge
on head; tall,
falcate fin; tall
columnar blow;
does not arch
back as much as
other whales or
raise flukes
when diving.
DIET
Broad range of
prey from small
schooling fish to
krill and
copepods.
BREEDING
Calves every 2–3
years; gestation
11–12 months.

The sei whale is poorly known. It lives far from shore, tends to be elusive and does not seem to gather in the same predictable areas year after year. There may be large numbers of sei whales in a particular region one year and then none for years or even decades afterwards. No commercial whale-watch operation relies on this species, for this reason, although it is sometimes encountered during tours specialising in humpbacks, minkes and other large whales. Named after a Norwegian word for the fish we call pollack, because the appearance of pollack off Norway's coast sometimes coincided with the arrival of sei whales, it is capable of swimming at up to 25 knots – making it one of the fastest of the large whales. For many years it was confused with the similar Bryde's whale, but the two species can be told apart by the number of longitudinal ridges along the tops of their heads.

Where to look

Found worldwide from tropical to cool temperate
waters. Most sei whales probably migrate between
cool summer feeding grounds and warm winter
breeding grounds. More than 200,000 were killed in
Antarctica in the past century and numbers there
remain greatly depleted. Unknown numbers were
killed elsewhere (whalers confused them with
Bryde's whales and anything vaguely resembling a
fin whale was often recorded merely as a 'finner').
Seis appear to be reasonably abundant in the North
Atlantic and North Pacific.

Fin Whale

Balaenoptera physalus

ID FACT FILE

OTHER NAMES
Finback, finner, herring whale, common rorqual, razorback.

MAXIMUM LENGTH
27 metres.

MAXIMUM WEIGHT
120 tonnes.

FIELD ID
Exceptionally large and sleek; dark upperside, light underside; asymmetrical head pigmentation; greyish-white chevron; small, backward-sloping fin far down back; single longitudinal ridge on head; tall, narrow blow; rarely raises flukes when diving.

DIET
Schooling fish, krill and other crustaceans, some squid (mainly krill in southern hemisphere).

BREEDING
Calves every 2–3 years; gestation 11–12 months

The second largest animal on Earth, after the blue whale, the fin whale is a sleek and fast swimmer capable of reaching speeds of over 25 knots. It is unusual in having asymmetrical pigmentation on its head – the lower jaw, mouth cavity and some of the baleen plates are white on the right side, but they are uniformly grey or black on the left side. No one knows the reason for such intriguing colouration, but it may be an adaptation to confuse the whale's small prey. Females are up to 10

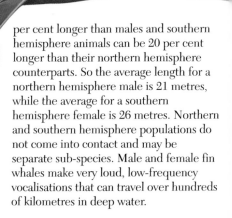

per cent longer than males and southern hemisphere animals can be 20 per cent longer than their northern hemisphere counterparts. So the average length for a northern hemisphere male is 21 metres, while the average for a southern hemisphere female is 26 metres. Northern and southern hemisphere populations do not come into contact and may be separate sub-species. Male and female fin whales make very loud, low-frequency vocalisations that can travel over hundreds of kilometres in deep water.

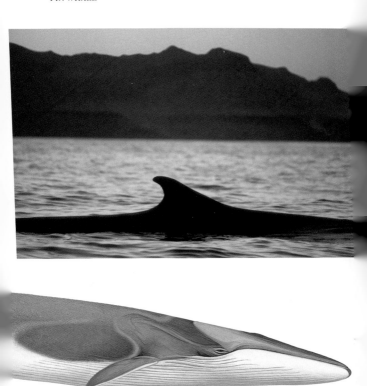

Where to look

Found in tropical, temperate and polar regions worldwide, but most common in cooler waters offshore. Some populations seem to be resident year-round, or make very short migrations, but others travel between warm waters in winter and cooler waters in summer. No distinct breeding or calving grounds have been identified. The world population was substantially reduced by commercial whaling (three-quarters of a million were killed in the southern hemisphere alone).

Blue Whale
Balaenoptera musculus

ID FACT FILE

OTHER NAMES
Sulphur-bottom,
Sibbald's rorqual,
great northern
rorqual.

MAXIMUM LENGTH
33.6 metres.

MAXIMUM WEIGHT
190 tonnes.

FIELD ID
Exceptionally
large; mottled
blue-grey; tiny,
stubby fin far
down back;
broad, flattened,
U-shaped head;
huge blowhole
splashguard;
single
longitudinal
ridge on head;
extremely thick
tailstock; very
tall blow; often
raises flukes
when diving.

DIET
Mainly krill,
occasionally
pelagic crabs.

BREEDING
Calves every 2–3
years; gestation
about 11
months.

The largest animal known to have lived on Earth, the blue whale is almost as long as a Boeing 737 and needs so much food that, in terms of weight, it could eat a fully-grown African elephant every day. But its sheer size made it one of the most sought-after species during the heyday of whaling and it was hunted relentlessly from the late nineteenth century until beyond the middle of the twentieth century. No fewer than 360,000 were killed in Antarctic waters alone. Some populations were reduced by 99 per cent of their original numbers and it is likely that they will never recover. Blue whales possess the loudest voice in the animal kingdom, emitting low-frequency sounds that can travel literally hundreds of kilometres in deep water. It is not known whether these are for long-distance communication or to assist with navigation and orientation. There is a sub-species known as the pygmy blue whale, which is particularly common in the Indian Ocean and may ultimately be recognised as a separate species.

Where to look
Worldwide from the tropics to the poles, although its distribution is very patchy. Some populations migrate long distances between low-latitude winter breeding grounds and high-latitude summer feeding grounds, but others appear to be resident. The only population that may be thriving today summers off the coasts of California and Mexico.

Sperm Whale

Physeter macrocephalus

ID FACT FILE

OTHER NAMES
Cachalot, great
sperm whale.
MAXIMUM LENGTH
11 metres
(female), 18
metres (male).
MAXIMUM WEIGHT
24 tonnes
(female), 57
tonnes (male).
FIELD ID
Dark body with
wrinkled skin;
huge, squarish
head; low hump
instead of fin;
'knuckles' from
hump to flukes;
single, slit-like
blowhole;
sideways,
forward-angled
blow; often lies
stationary at
surface; raises
flukes high when
diving.
DIET
Mainly squid, but
also octopuses,
sharks and other
fish.
BREEDING
Calves every 4–6
years (longer in
older females);
gestation 14–18
months.

With its disproportionately large head
and wrinkled skin, the sperm whale is
very distinctive. The largest of the
toothed whales, it dives deeper and for
longer than any other cetacean (with the
possible exception of some beaked
whales). No other cetacean shows such a
marked difference in size between the
sexes: males are almost twice as large as
females and lead very different lives.
Groups of females and immatures of both
sexes stay in the same general area for
many years, but adult males are generally
solitary and travel huge distances. In fact,
the males travel so far and wide that
populations around the world are very
similar genetically. The sperm whale was
the mainstay of the whaling industry for
many years, hunted mainly for its
spermaceti oil (a waxy oil found in the
head) and body oil. It is believed that
more than a million sperm whales were
killed over several centuries and the latest
population estimate suggests there could
be as few as 360,000 left.

Where to look

Patchy distribution worldwide from the tropics to high latitudes near the edge of the pack ice. Sperm whales are most common offshore and over deepwater canyons, but can be found close to shore if the water is sufficiently deep. Most females and immature males live in temperate and tropical seas at latitudes less than 40° (50° in the North Pacific). Only the large adult males venture to the extreme north and south of the range, where they feed.

THE WHALE THAT THINKS IT IS A SUBMARINE

Sperm whales behave more like submarines than air-breathing mammals. Capable of diving well beyond the limits of almost any other mammal, they disappear into the cold, dark ocean depths to catch deepwater squid or sharks and other large fish.

They eat as much as a tonne of food every day, each prey animal ranging in size from a few centimetres to almost the length of the whales themselves. One individual was observed tackling a giant squid some 14.5 metres long, including its tentacles, while no fewer than 28,000 smaller squid were found in the stomach of another.

Scientists from the Woods Hole Oceanographic Institute recorded an incredible, record-breaking dive during a research study near the Caribbean island of Dominica. In 1991, they tagged a pair of male sperm whales and regularly tracked them at depths of 400–600 metres. On one occasion, though, the larger of the two whales made a breathtaking dive to a depth of 2,000 metres.

There is plenty of circumstantial evidence to suggest that sperm whales may be able to dive even deeper. On 25 August 1969, for example, a male sperm whale was killed by whalers 160 kilometres south of Durban, South Africa.

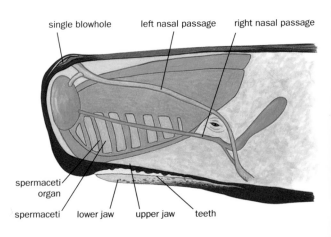

single blowhole   left nasal passage   right nasal passage

spermaceti organ

spermaceti   lower jaw   upper jaw   teeth

SPERM WHALE

Inside its stomach were two small sharks which, according to local experts, had been swallowed about an hour earlier; these were later identified as a particular kind of dogfish, found only on the seafloor. Since the water in that area exceeds a depth of 3,193 metres for a radius of some 48–64 kilometres, it is logical to assume that the sperm whale had been to a similar depth when hunting the two sharks.

Incidentally, the same whale also made one of the longest confirmed dives of any mammal. By the time it surfaced to breathe, having caught its prey, it had been underwater for an incredible one hour 52 minutes.

One explanation for such astonishing diving capabilities may lie in the sperm whale's enormous, barrel-shaped head. Much of the bulk of the head consists of a strange spongy tissue, known as the spermaceti organ, which is saturated with a yellowy wax. According to one theory, this could be used to control the whale's buoyancy in the water. By altering the temperature (and thus the density) of the wax the whale could sink or float with the minimum of effort. Another idea is that it cushions the animal's head during fights (heavy scarring and occasional broken teeth and jaws suggest serious skirmishes between males). But the most likely theory to explain the purpose of this massive oil-filled organ is that it works as an acoustic lens to channel sound emissions.

Dwarf Sperm Whale

Kogia sima

ID FACT FILE

OTHER NAMES
Owen's pygmy
sperm whale.
MAXIMUM LENGTH
2.7 metres.
MAXIMUM WEIGHT
275 kilograms.
FIELD ID
Small, robust
body; bluish-grey
upperside, dull
white or pinkish
underside;
squarish head
with underslung
lower jaw;
prominent,
falcate fin
midway along
back; false
'gill'; low,
inconspicuous
blow; floats
motionless at
surface; does
not raise flukes
when diving.
DIET
Mainly mid- and
deep-water
squid, some fish
and crustaceans.
BREEDING
May calve every
2 years or less;
gestation about
12 months.

Like their much larger and better-known
relative, dwarf sperm whales have
spermaceti organs in their heads and are
deep divers. They are very similar in
appearance to pygmy sperm whales and
the two species are difficult to tell apart at
sea, except in perfect conditions at very
close range. They were separated as
distinct species as recently as 1966. The
dwarf sperm whale is slightly smaller (by
about half a metre on average) and usually
has a more prominent dorsal fin
positioned farther forward on the back.
Stranded individuals of both species
have been mistaken for sharks
because of their
underslung lower
jaws and the
distinctive
crescent-shaped
markings on
either side of the head between the eye
and the flipper (which resemble gill-slits
and have been dubbed 'false gills'). Dwarf
sperm whales occur alone or in small
groups of up to 10 animals of mixed age
and sex. Both species are often seen lying
motionless at the surface, with the back of
the head exposed and the tail hanging
down in the water. They can be
approached quite closely, but then startle
and dive.

DWARF SPERM WHALE

Where to look
Dwarf sperm whales are found worldwide in tropical
to temperate waters of the Atlantic, Pacific and
Indian Oceans, although they have never been
officially recorded across vast areas within this
assumed range. Some evidence suggests that the
dwarf sperm whale may prefer warmer, shallower
coastal waters than the pygmy sperm whale. There is
no evidence that the species migrates.

Pygmy Sperm Whale
Kogia breviceps

ID FACT FILE

OTHER NAMES
Lesser sperm whale, short-headed sperm whale, lesser cachalot.

MAXIMUM LENGTH
3.8 metres.

MAXIMUM WEIGHT
450 kilograms.

FIELD ID
Small, robust body; bluish-grey upperside, dull white or pinkish underside; squarish head with underslung lower jaw; falcate fin behind midline on body; false 'gill'; low, inconspicuous blow; floats motionless at surface; does not raise flukes when diving.

DIET
Mainly mid- and deep-water squid, some fish and crustaceans.

BREEDING
May calve every 2 years or less; gestation about 12 months.

Like the virtually identical dwarf sperm whale, the pygmy sperm whale is rarely encountered at sea except in a few well-known hotspots. Neither species appears to be particularly numerous, although they can be overlooked in anything but the calmest conditions and may be more common than the lack of evidence currently suggests. Both species are sometimes killed in Japan, Indonesia and the Lesser Antilles, and at least some are drowned in fishing nets. They are unusual among cetaceans in having a store of dark reddish-brown liquid in the lower intestines, which they expel into the water when they are startled – perhaps as a decoy, like the ink of a squid. They also have unusually-

shaped heads, which appear square from the side
and conical when viewed from above or below;
they become blunter and squarer as the animals
age. Pygmy sperm whales occur alone or in small
groups of up to six animals of mixed age and sex.

Where to look

Pygmy sperm whales are found worldwide in
tropical to temperate waters of the Atlantic, Pacific
and Indian Oceans, although they have never been
officially recorded across vast areas within this
assumed range. Limited evidence suggests that the
pygmy sperm whale prefers cooler, deeper waters
seaward of the continental shelf. There is no
evidence that the species migrates.

Narwhal
Monodon monoceros

ID FACT FILE

OTHER NAMES
Narwhale.
MAXIMUM LENGTH
4.7 metres.
MAXIMUM WEIGHT
1.6 tonnes.
FIELD ID
Long tusk of male; mottled black-and-white back and sides; low fleshy ridge instead of fin; short, rounded head; slight hint of beak; short, upcurled flippers; convex 'backward-facing' flukes; inhabits very high latitudes; rarely raises flukes when diving.
DIET
Variety of fish, squid and crustaceans.
BREEDING
Calves every 2–3 years; gestation about 15 months.

Centuries ago the male narwhal's long, spiralling tusk was believed to be the horn of the legendary unicorn and traders selling it made huge profits by keeping this distinctive whale's existence a secret. Looking like a gnarled and twisted walking stick, the tusk is actually a modified tooth – the left of two upper teeth, it pierces the lip and keeps growing to a length of up to three metres. A small number of males have two tusks and, rarely, females grow them as well. Their purpose is still a matter of debate, but they are certainly not used to spear fish and may instead be weapons in fights over females or used as visual displays of strength. Narwhals are deep divers, capable of staying underwater for as long as 20 minutes and reaching depths of more than 1,000 metres. They have been hunted for centuries by indigenous peoples for their meat and tusks and in some areas are threatened by oil and gas exploration and pollution. The total population is believed to be around 50,000.

Where to look

A truly Arctic species, the narwhal lives further north than almost any other cetacean. Found mostly above the Arctic Circle, and right to the edge of the permanent ice, it moves with the receding and expanding ice edge. It is most common on the North Atlantic side of the Arctic (especially Greenland and north-western Canada) and less common on the North Pacific side.

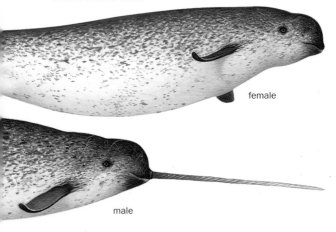

female

male

Beluga
Delphinapterus leucas

ID FACT FILE

OTHER NAMES
Belukha, sea
canary, white
whale.
MAXIMUM LENGTH
4.9 metres.
MAXIMUM WEIGHT
1.6 tonnes.
FIELD ID
White adult body
colour; small
head with
rounded melon;
flexible neck;
narrow dorsal
ridge instead of
fin; extremely
short beak;
broad mouthline;
dark fringes to
ridge, flippers
and flukes;
frequently
spyhops; no
acrobatics; high
latitudes.
DIET
Variety of fish,
squid,
octopuses,
crustaceans and
marine worms.
BREEDING
Calves every 3
years; gestation
about 11–14
months.

Ancient mariners used to call the
beluga the 'sea canary' because of its
great repertoire of trills, moos, clicks,
squeaks and twitters, which was once
described by a beluga scientist as
sounding like a string orchestra tuning
up before a concert. One of the most
vocal of all the toothed whales, it can
even be heard from above the surface.
Unlike most other cetaceans, it can
change the shape of its extraordinary
bulging head and is able to turn its head
from side to side or move it up and
down. Not all belugas are white: the
body colour changes with age, from
dark slate-grey at birth to pure white
(with dark lines along the dorsal ridge
and the edges of the flippers and flukes)

in adulthood. Known to dive to depths of at least 800 metres, belugas are believed to forage near the seabed. They have been hunted for centuries and pollution is a serious threat in some regions. The best population estimate is around 100,000.

Where to look

Belugas are found only in seasonally ice-covered waters of the sub-Arctic and Arctic. They occur mostly in shallow coastal waters, but will enter estuaries and even rivers. The largest population (accounting for 40 per cent of the total) lives in the Beaufort Sea, but they are more readily seen in eastern Canada's lower St Lawrence River and the Churchill River in western Hudson Bay.

BEAKED WHALES

The beaked whales are the strangest and least known of all the cetaceans. Several of them have never been seen alive and the only evidence of their existence has been gleaned from dead animals caught by fishermen or washed ashore. Others are known from just a few brief encounters at sea, but have never been photographed. Very few have been studied in any detail.

There are currently 21 known species, all belonging to the family Ziphiidae. But this figure is constantly under review as new species are discovered and described. The most recent addition to the list is Perrin's beaked whale, which was formally named in 2002 and is known from just five animals stranded along the coast of California. Another relatively new species is Bahamonde's beaked whale, which was added to the list in 1995; also known as the spade-toothed whale, this whale was described from nothing more than part of a skull found in the Juan Fernández Islands, off the coast of Chile.

Beaked whales are small- to medium-sized whales, ranging in length from just under four metres to nearly 13 metres. As their name suggests, the majority of them have pronounced beaks, which are relatively shorter than in most dolphins but longer than in most whales. They also have a pair of distinctive throat grooves (in the shape of a 'V') and, unique among cetaceans, slight depressions called 'flipper pockets' where their small flippers can be tucked away alongside the body.

But their most remarkable feature is their teeth. There are no functional teeth in females or immature males (they do not erupt or are absent altogether) and there are only two or four functional teeth in the lower jaw of adult males. Shepherd's beaked whale is the main exception: both sexes have a full set of normal odontocete teeth in both the upper and lower jaws. Also, tiny teeth are present in the upper jaw of both sexes in Gray's beaked whales (embedded in the gum rather than the bone).

Observing and identifying beaked whales at sea can be extremely difficult. They usually live far from land and spend relatively little time at the surface between dives. More frustratingly, many species look remarkably alike from a distance. Relying on colour alone is virtually impossible for most species, since so little is known about the colouration of live animals and the little we do know suggests that there is tremendous variation between individuals. Normally there is

no visible blow, and no beaked whales are known to lift their flukes when diving. In many cases, females are impossible to identify positively at sea unless they are accompanied by males.

However, more researchers have made an effort to study the enigmatic beaked whales in recent years and, although they are still shrouded in mystery, our knowledge has improved enormously.

Peruvian beaked whale skull

Sowerby's Beaked Whale

Mesoplodon bidens

ID FACT FILE

OTHER NAMES
North Sea
beaked whale,
North Atlantic
beaked whale.
MAXIMUM LENGTH
5.5 metres.
MAXIMUM WEIGHT
1.3 tonnes.
FIELD ID
(Male only)
Bluish-grey or
slate-grey
upperside, lighter
underside; teeth
mid-way along
long, slender
beak; slight
bulge in front of
blowhole; small
falcate fin two-
thirds of the way
along back;
limited scarring;
usually
unobtrusive
behaviour;
surfaces at
steep angle.
DIET
Squid and some
fish.
BREEDING
Calving interval
and gestation
period unknown.

Sowerby's beaked whale was the first of the beaked whales to be described – a male stranded in 1800 in the Moray Firth, north-eastern Scotland, and the skull was collected. A couple of years later, James Sowerby, an English watercolour artist, painted a picture of the skull and how he imagined the animal might have looked. Although its existence has been known for over two centuries, Sowerby's beaked whale is rarely encountered at sea and is still poorly known. It does occasionally strand, but basic natural history data such as stomach contents is still limited. The position of the teeth in the male is distinctive, lying mid-way between the tip of the beak and the corner of the

female

mouth, although they may be visible only at close range. Females are probably unidentifiable at sea. They are usually seen alone or in small groups of up to 10 animals of mixed sex and age and are capable of diving for at least half an hour.

Where to look

With one of the most northerly distributions of all beaked whales, this species is found mainly in cold temperate and sub-arctic waters of the northern North Atlantic. It appears to be most common in the east, especially in the northern North Sea. There are no known hunts, although Sowerby's beaked whale has been hunted in the past off Iceland and in the Barents Sea. Nothing is known about its abundance.

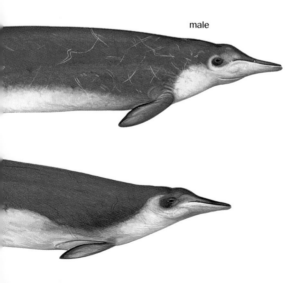

male

Andrews' Beaked Whale

Mesoplodon bowdoini

ID FACT FILE

OTHER NAMES
Bowdoin's beaked whale, splay-toothed beaked whale, deepcrest beaked whale.

MAXIMUM LENGTH
4.9 metres.

MAXIMUM WEIGHT
Possibly 1.5 tonnes.

FIELD ID
(Male only)
Robust body; dark blue-black colour; white scratches and scars; short, thick beak predominantly white; strongly arched mouthline; teeth visible in middle of beak; small fin.

DIET
Probably squid and some fish.

BREEDING
Calving interval and gestation period unknown.

Andrews' beaked whale is so similar in appearance and morphology to Hubbs' beaked whale that it has been suggested they belong to the same species. However, based on genetic evidence they are currently considered to be distinct species. Andrews' has never been

male

positively identified at sea, so everything we know about it has been inferred from strandings. These are relatively infrequent, suggesting that it is relatively rare. The male, in particular, is rather distinctive with a short, thick beak and a large tooth perched on the top of each side of its highly arched lower jaw. Linear body scarring on adult males is probably made by the teeth of other males. The species is named after a curator at the American Museum of Natural History in New York, Roy Chapman Andrews.

Where to look

Known only from strandings along the southern coast of Australia (including Tasmania) and New Zealand (including some sub-Antarctic islands), as well as oceanic islands such as the Falkland Islands and Tristan da Cunha. Such limited evidence suggests that Andrews' beaked whale has a circumpolar distribution in the southern hemisphere north of the Antarctic Convergence.

Hubbs' Beaked Whale

Mesoplodon carlhubbsi

Hubbs' beaked whale is another poorly-known member of the family and, again, most information comes from strandings. Adult males are covered in a remarkable number of single and double linear scars, which are probably made by the teeth of other males during aggressive encounters over females or dominance hierarchies. Other male beaked whales have similar scarring, but rarely as much as in this species. It is so similar in appearance and morphology to Andrews' beaked whale

ID FACT FILE

OTHER NAMES
Arch-beaked whale.
MAXIMUM LENGTH
5.3 metres.
MAXIMUM WEIGHT
1.5 tonnes.
FIELD ID
(Male only) Dark, robust body; tangle of linear scars; raised white 'cap' on fairly bulbous melon; stocky, elongated beak mainly white; strongly arched lower jaw; massive teeth visible on top of arch in centre of beak; slightly falcate fin.
DIET
Squid and some fish.
BREEDING
Calving interval and gestation period unknown.

male

that it has been suggested they belong to the same species. However, based on genetic evidence, they are currently considered to be distinct. Hubbs' beaked whale was named after the American ichthyologist Carl Hubbs – in 1945, a live specimen stranded outside his office at Scripps Institution of Oceanography, in California.

Where to look

Known only from temperate waters in the North Pacific, Hubbs' beaked whale appears to be most common along the California coast and north into British Columbia. It may occur as far south as the Pacific coast of Baja California, Mexico. However, it has also been recorded in Japan (along the north-eastern coast of the main island of Honshu) and therefore may range right across the North Pacific.

Blainville's Beaked Whale

Mesoplodon densirostris

ID FACT FILE

OTHER NAMES
Tropical beaked
whale, dense-
beaked whale,
Atlantic beaked
whale.
MAXIMUM LENGTH
4.9 metres.
MAXIMUM WEIGHT
1 tonne.
FIELD ID
(Male only) Dark
upperside, lighter
underside; fairly
prominent fin
two-thirds of the
way along back;
strongly-arched
lower jaw; thick,
moderately long
beak; huge, horn-
like teeth;
flattened
forehead; many
oval scars, some
scratching.
DIET
Squid and
octopuses.
BREEDING
Calving interval
and gestation
period unknown.

Blainville's beaked whale has a wider
distribution than almost any other known
beaked whale, but sightings are still
relatively rare. Most of our knowledge
comes from dead animals washed ashore
– it often strands on oceanic islands on
both sides of the equator – and from
observations on live animals in just three
key hotspots. However, it was one of the
first beaked whales to be identified
when, in 1817, Henri de Blainville
managed to describe it from a small piece
of jaw. His specimen was the heaviest
bone structure he had ever seen (denser
even than elephant ivory) and this gave
rise to its other common name: the
dense-beaked whale. The male has a
distinctive, high-arched
jawline, with two
large teeth on
the crest
that grow
forward and
protrude from
both sides of the closed
mouth. The teeth are not always

female

visible, though, as they can be obscured by stalked barnacles. Blainville's beaked whales make deep dives for food that can last for up to 45 minutes.

Where to look

Mainly found in tropical to warm temperate waters worldwide, especially in deep water and around gullies on the continental slope. Occasional records in higher latitudes may be linked to warm water currents. There are only three areas where Blainville's beaked whale is observed on a regular basis: the north-eastern Bahamas; Oahu, Hawaii; and Moorea in the Society Islands of the South Pacific.

male

Perrin's Beaked Whale

Mesoplodon perrini

ID FACT FILE

OTHER NAMES
None.
MAXIMUM LENGTH
4.4 metres.
MAXIMUM WEIGHT
Unknown.
FIELD ID
(Male only) Dark
grey above, pale
underneath;
relatively small
size; spindle-
shaped body;
some scarring;
small bulge at
melon; short
beak, pale grey or
white; triangular
teeth near tip of
lower jaw; small
dorsal fin.
DIET
Probably squid
and some fish.
BREEDING
Calving interval
and gestation
period unknown.

Perrin's beaked whale is the most recent addition to the cetacean list, and was described for the first time in 2002. It is known from just five animals which stranded along the coast of California between 1975 and 1997. There was considerable confusion over their identification at first, and four were initially identified as Hector's beaked whales and the fifth as Cuvier's beaked whale. However, after detailed genetic studies, beaked whale experts realised they belonged to a new species. It now seems likely that sightings of two small beaked whales off California in 1976 and 1978, which were identified as Hector's beaked whales, are more likely to have been Perrin's. There are subtle differences between the two species. Perrin's beaked whale was named after W. F. Perrin, who collected two of the known specimens.

male

Where to look

Known only from five strandings in California, between Torrey Pines State Reserve just north of San Diego and Fisherman's Wharf in Monterey, suggesting a range in the eastern North Pacific. However, this is very limited evidence and it is possible that the true distribution is much broader. Like other beaked whales, it is likely to be found in oceanic waters deeper than 1,000 metres.

Hector's Beaked Whale

Mesoplodon hectori

Until recently, information about Hector's beaked whale was confusing. It was known mostly from stranded animals in two widely separated parts of the world: in the southern hemisphere and many thousands of kilometres away along the coast of California. But the four animals stranded in California between 1975 and 1997 (originally identified as Hector's beaked whales) are now known to be a recently-described species,

male

Perrin's beaked whale. Hector's beaked whale has never been reliably identified alive in the wild. Very little is known about its abundance, but it is generally considered to be one of the rarer beaked whales. Like Hector's dolphin, this species was named after the curator of the colonial museum in Wellington, New Zealand: Sir James Hector.

ID FACT FILE

OTHER NAMES
New Zealand beaked whale, skew-beaked whale.

MAXIMUM LENGTH
4.2 metres.

MAXIMUM WEIGHT
Unknown.

FIELD ID
(Male only) Dark upperside, lighter underside; small, spindle-shaped body; large, slightly triangular teeth on tip of lower jaw; small, triangular and slightly falcate dorsal fin two-thirds of the way along back.

DIET
Probably squid and some fish.

BREEDING
Calving interval and gestation period unknown.

Where to look

Most records of Hector's beaked whale are from New Zealand, but it seems to have a circumpolar distribution in cool, temperate waters of the southern hemisphere. There are also records from Chile, Argentina, the Falkland Islands, South Africa and Tasmania. Earlier records of Hector's beaked whales in the northern hemisphere are now known to be Perrin's beaked whale.

Gervais' Beaked Whale
Mesoplodon europaeus

ID FACT FILE

OTHER NAMES
Gulf Stream beaked whale, Antillean beaked whale, European beaked whale.

MAXIMUM LENGTH
5.2 metres.

MAXIMUM WEIGHT
1.5 tonnes.

FIELD ID
(Male only) Medium-sized, slender body; dark grey upperside, paler grey underside; spindle-shaped body; some linear scarring; fairly long, narrow beak; teeth barely visible a third of the way back from tip of jaw; small fin two-thirds of the way down back.

DIET
Probably squid and some fish.

BREEDING
Calving interval and gestation period unknown.

Gervais' beaked whale is another poorly-known member of the family that has never been reliably identified alive at sea. Consequently, nearly everything we know about its distribution, abundance and natural history has been gleaned from a relatively small number of strandings. The type specimen (used to describe the species) was found floating dead in the English Channel in 1840 – hence it was scientifically named *Mesoplodon europaeus* in 1855 and, for a while at least, dubbed the European beaked whale. However, most records are from warmer waters further south, along the Atlantic coast of North America, in the

Caribbean and in the Gulf of Mexico. Intriguingly, a count of tooth layers in one particular stranded individual suggests that it was at least 27 years old.

Where to look
Deep tropical and warm temperate waters in the western North Atlantic, with scattered records in the eastern North Atlantic: western Africa, the Canary Islands and Ireland. It is also known from Ascension Island, in the South Atlantic. There is no information on its abundance, although it does strand along the Atlantic coast of North America (especially in Florida) more than any other *Mesoplodon* species.

male

female

Ginkgo-toothed Beaked Whale

Mesoplodon ginkgodens

ID FACT FILE

OTHER NAMES
Ginkgo beaked
whale, Japanese
beaked whale.
MAXIMUM LENGTH
4.9 metres.
MAXIMUM WEIGHT
Unknown.
FIELD ID
(Male only)
Relatively small,
robust body; dark
upperside,
possibly lighter
underside; little
or no linear
scarring; white
spots and
blotches;
smoothly-sloping
forehead; arched
lower jaw; teeth
barely visible on
arch; small fin
two-thirds of the
way along back.
DIET
Probably
squid

and
some fish.
BREEDING
Calving interval
and gestation
period unknown.

The ginkgo-toothed beaked whale is
named for the male's strangely flattened
teeth, which are shaped like the leaves of
a ginkgo tree – a common tree in Japan,
where the first specimen of this whale
was found and described in 1958. These
teeth are about 10 centimetres wide,
making them the widest of any known
Mesoplodon species. The ginkgo-toothed
beaked whale has never been identified
alive at sea and is very poorly known.
Most information comes from stranded
animals found on shore and a handful of
individuals killed by Japanese whalers.
Unlike many of its relatives, the male has
very few (if any) linear scars
on its body – suggesting
that males do not
fight over

dominance hierarchies or females. However, males do have white spots and blotches, especially around the navel, which may be parasitic scars rather than true pigmentation.

Where to look

This species is known only from a small number of widely-scattered records in the tropical and warm temperate waters of the Pacific and Indian Oceans, from Japan and California to the Galapagos Islands and the Maldives. The ginkgo-toothed beaked whale was being hunted on an opportunistic basis by shore-based whalers in Japan and Taiwan even before it had been scientifically described. There is no information on abundance.

male

Gray's Beaked Whale

Mesoplodon grayi

ID FACT FILE

OTHER NAMES
Haast's beaked
whale,
scamperdown
whale, southern
beaked whale,
small-toothed
beaked whale.

MAXIMUM LENGTH
5.6 metres.

MAXIMUM WEIGHT
1.3 tonnes.

FIELD ID
(Male only)
Slender, spindle-
shaped body;
dark upperside,
lighter underside;
very long,
slender,
predominantly
white beak;
slightly bulging
melon; small,
triangular teeth
visible about a
third of way back
from tip of beak;
small, falcate fin
two-thirds of the
way along back.

DIET
Probably squid
and some fish.

BREEDING
Calving interval
and gestation
period unknown.

Gray's beaked whales are among the
better-known *Mesoplodon* species.
Named in 1876 after John Edward Gray,
a zoologist at the British Museum, they
seem to be more active at the surface
than other beaked whales and are among
the few that have been photographed
alive at sea. This species is unique in the
Mesoplodon genus because adults of both
sexes have 34–44 tiny, evenly-spaced
teeth in the upper jaw. Adult males also
have two teeth on the lower jaw. Like the
other beaked whales with especially long
beaks, they often lift their beaks out of
the water at an angle of about 45 degrees
when surfacing. Although
normally encountered
or stranded

in small groups of up to eight animals, in 1874 there was a mass stranding of 28 in the Chatham Islands, east of New Zealand. This species is believed to be one of the most gregarious members of the family.

Where to look
Gray's beaked whale has a circumpolar distribution in temperate waters of the southern hemisphere, mainly in the Southern Ocean south of 30°S. There is a single record from the northern hemisphere – a stranding in the Netherlands in 1927 – but this is believed to have been exceptional and well outside the normal range. The high number of strandings suggests that it is fairly common and widespread.

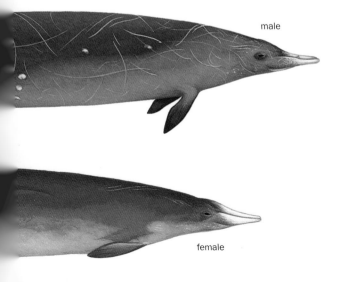

male

female

Strap-toothed Whale

Mesoplodon layardii

ID FACT FILE

OTHER NAMES
Layard's beaked
whale.
MAXIMUM LENGTH
6.2 metres.
MAXIMUM WEIGHT
1.5 tonnes.
FIELD ID
(Male only)
Strong dark and
light markings;
considerable
body scarring;
small fin two-
thirds of the way
along back; teeth
curled around
upper jaw; long,
slender beak;
slightly bulging
melon; dark face
'mask'; beak
may break
surface first;
difficult to
approach.
DIET
Squid.
BREEDING
Calving interval
and gestation
period unknown.

The male strap-toothed whale is the
largest member of the *Mesoplodon*
genus. It has two extraordinary teeth
which grow from its lower jaw, curl
upwards and backwards and then extend
over the top of its upper jaw. In older
animals, they sometimes meet in the
middle, forming a muzzle and
preventing the whale from opening its
jaws more than a few centimetres. The
teeth may act as 'guard-rails', helping
the whale to catch squid, its main prey,
while it uses its mouth to suck like a
vacuum cleaner. But this would not
explain why such 'wrap-around' teeth
are absent in females. A more likely
explanation is that the teeth are a sexual
characteristic, perhaps used in fighting

or in some other way to determine the fittest males for mating. The variety of tooth formations originally led to the naming of at least four new species, but scientists now recognise that they are in fact all the same species. The strap-toothed whale was described by John Edward Gray, in 1865, from drawings sent by a curator of the South African Museum called E. L. Layard – thus its alternative name.

Where to look
The strap-toothed whale has a wide distribution in cool temperate waters of the southern hemisphere, roughly between 30°S and the Antarctic Convergence. It has stranded on beaches in Chile, Argentina, Uruguay, the Falkland Islands, southern Africa, New Zealand and Australia; although poorly known, it appears to be relatively common.

male

Stejneger's Beaked Whale
Mesoplodon stejnegeri

For nearly a century, the only evidence for the existence of Stejneger's beaked whale came from a single skull found on Bering Island, in the mid-nineteenth century. But since the late 1970s information about this enigmatic whale has improved and there are now more specimens available for study. In particular, in 1994 a group of four adult females stranded in the Aleutian Islands –

providing the first Stejneger's beaked whales in good condition. The male has extraordinary tusk-like teeth, second only in size to the teeth of strap-toothed whales, which are set about 20 centimetres from the tip of the jaw immediately in front of the apex. They are laterally compressed and tilt forwards, sometimes converging towards one another and cutting into the upper lip. The species was named in 1855 after the man who found the first skull, Leonhard Stejneger.

Where to look
Cool temperate and sub-arctic waters of the North
Pacific (from California to Japan) and in the south-
western Bering Sea. Stejneger's may also range into
warm temperate waters, but the only evidence
for this is the presence of scars inflicted by cookie-
cutter sharks (the sharks are more abundant in
warmer waters further south).

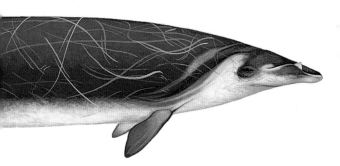

The Aleutian Islands may be a key centre of
distribution and there appears to be a distinct
population in the Sea of Japan.

Pygmy Beaked Whale

Mesoplodon peruvianus

ID FACT FILE

OTHER NAMES
Peruvian beaked
whale, lesser
beaked whale.

MAXIMUM LENGTH
3.9 metres.

MAXIMUM WEIGHT
Unknown.

FIELD ID
(Male only) Small
size; spindle-
shaped body;
dark upperside,
lighter underside;
linear scarring;
slightly bulbous
melon; slightly
sloping forehead;
small beak with
slightly arched
jaw; teeth just
visible in front of
arch; small,
triangular fin two-
thirds of the way
along back.

DIET
Fish and
probably squid.

BREEDING
Calving interval
and gestation
period unknown.

The pygmy beaked whale is the smallest
member of the family and one of the
most recent cetacean species to be
named. Scientists first became aware of
its existence in 1976, when a skull was
discovered at a fish market near San
Andrés, in Peru. The first complete
specimen (a female) was found in 1985,
at another fish market just south of Lima,
in Peru, and the first adult male was
found three years later. In 1990, there
were two strandings in La Paz Bay, Baja
California, Mexico – the first
outside Peruvian waters.
The new species was
officially named in
1991. Since then, it has
been reliably identified
at sea on several occasions, but almost
nothing is known about its social structure
or behaviour. There is also no information
on abundance, but because many of the
first specimens had been caught by
fishermen off the coast of Peru, it raises
alarm bells about what appears to be a
high level of incidental catch.

Where to look
Limited records suggest mid- to deep waters in the eastern tropical and temperate Pacific, mainly off the coasts of Peru and Chile, but extending from northern Mexico or southern California to northern Chile. However, the range may be more extensive as there is also a possible record – a stranding – from New Zealand.

female

male

Bahamonde's Beaked Whale
Mesoplodon traversii

ID FACT FILE

OTHER NAMES
Spade-toothed
whale.

MAXIMUM LENGTH
Possibly 5.5
metres (based
on skull size).

MAXIMUM WEIGHT
Unknown.

FIELD ID
Similarities
in skull
characteristics
suggest that it
may be closely
related to
Andrews' beaked
whale and,
consequently, may
be similar in
appearance.

DIET
Probably squid
and fish.

BREEDING
Calving interval
and gestation
period unknown.

Part of a strange skull, belonging to an immature beaked whale, was found on Robinson Crusoe Island, in the Juan Fernández islands off Chile, in June 1986. After nearly a decade of painstaking examination by some of the world's leading beaked whale experts, it was officially named in 1995 as a species new to science. Since then, it has been discovered that two more specimens (part of a skull from New Zealand and an old tooth and jaw from the Chatham Islands) are genetically identical to the Chilean skull. It is possible that Bahamonde's beaked whale and the so-called 'unidentified beaked whale', known only from sightings in the Eastern Tropical Pacific, belong to the same species – but until complete specimens are found this is merely conjecture. The scientific name has recently been changed from *Mesoplodon bahamondi*.

Bahamonde's beaked
whale skull

Where to look
Currently known only from the Juan Fernández Archipelago, some 590 kilometres to the west of mainland Chile, and New Zealand (including the Chatham Islands). This would suggest a range across the South Pacific, but there is far too little evidence to be certain.

Shepherd's Beaked Whale

Tasmacetus shepherdi

Shepherd's beaked whale is the only member of the family with a full set of functional teeth in both jaws (Gray's beaked whale has tiny, vestigial teeth in the upper jaw). These occur in both sexes, though only the male has a pair of enlarged teeth at the tip of the lower jaw as in other beaked whales. Since most records are based on partly-decomposed animals washed ashore, there is little information on its appearance.

male

Shepherd's beaked whale was described by W. B. B. Oliver in 1937 from a nearly complete skeleton collected by a curator at the Wanganui Alexander Museum in New Zealand, G. Shepherd.

Where to look

Shepherd's beaked whales are known from strandings in New Zealand, the Chatham Islands, Australia, Argentina, the Juan Fernández Islands off Chile, Tristan da Cunha and the South Sandwich Islands. More than half of these were in New Zealand. Assuming that a sighting in the Seychelles was exceptional, this limited evidence suggests that it may be circumpolar in cool temperate waters between 33°S and 50°S.

ID FACT FILE

OTHER NAMES
Tasman beaked whale, Tasman whale.

MAXIMUM LENGTH
7 metres.

MAXIMUM WEIGHT
Unknown.

FIELD ID
(Male only)
Moderately large, spindle-shaped body; dark upperside, light patches on sides, underside and tail stock; light patch on bulbous melon; long, narrow, pointed beak with small teeth on tip; small, slightly falcate fin two-thirds of the way along back.

DIET
Probably squid and fish in equal quantities.

BREEDING
Calving interval and gestation period unknown.

Longman's Beaked Whale

Indopacetus pacificus

ID FACT FILE

OTHER NAMES
Pacific beaked whale, Indo-Pacific beaked whale.

MAXIMUM LENGTH
Possibly 8 metres (Maldivian female 5.9 metres).

MAXIMUM WEIGHT
Unknown.

FIELD ID
Relatively large size; brownish upperside, lighter underside; bulbous melon; visible low, bushy blow; moderately long, stubby beak; two teeth near tip of lower jaw (presumably erupting in male only); falcate fin two-thirds of the way along back.

DIET
Probably squid and fish.

BREEDING
Calving interval and gestation period unknown.

Until recently, Longman's beaked whale was one of the least-known cetaceans. The only evidence for its existence came from two weathered skulls: one discovered in 1882 on a beach near MacKay, in Queensland, Australia, and the other in 1955 on the floor of a fertiliser factory in Mogadishu, Somalia (later traced to a beach near Danane, where it had been picked up by a local fisherman). But in recent years four new specimens have been found: two juvenile males stranded on the Indian Ocean coast of South Africa, an adult female stranded in the Maldives, and a skull found in Kenya. Unfortunately, there is still no adult male available for study. However, in the past couple of years there have been some reliable

sightings of Longman's beaked whales at sea
(especially in the Maldives); and large beaked
whales occasionally reported from the warmer
waters of the Indian and Pacific Oceans – and
dubbed 'tropical bottlenose whales' – are now
believed to have been Longman's. The species is
named after Heber Longman, a curator at the
Queensland Museum, Australia, who recognised
the 1882 skull as belonging to a new species.

Where to look
Based on limited evidence from just six specimens
and a small number of reliable sightings at sea,
Longman's beaked whale appears to be distributed
in the western reaches of the tropical Pacific
Ocean and in the western, northern and southern
tropical Indian Ocean. 'Tropical bottlenose
whales' have been reported throughout the
tropical Indo-Pacific.

Cuvier's Beaked Whale

Ziphius cavirostris

ID FACT FILE

OTHER NAMES
Goose-beaked
whale.
MAXIMUM LENGTH
6.9 metres.
MAXIMUM WEIGHT
3 tonnes.
FIELD ID
(Male only)
Rotund body;
small head
shaped like
goose's beak;
white head;
small teeth at tip
of jaw; small,
falcate fin set
about two-thirds
along back; low,
inconspicuous
blow; long and
circular scars;
usually alone or
in small groups.
DIET
Mainly squid, but
sometimes fish
and possibly
crustaceans.
BREEDING
Calving interval
and gestation
period unknown.

When Cuvier's beaked whale was first
described by the French anatomist
Georges Cuvier, in 1823, it was believed
to be extinct. However, it is now known
to be one of the most abundant and
widespread of the beaked whales and is
one of the three most-watched members
of the family (along with Baird's beaked
whale and the northern bottlenose
whale). The shape of its head and beak is
sometimes described as resembling a
goose's beak, which explains its
alternative name, the goose-beaked
whale. Cuvier's beaked whales vary
enormously in colour, but are among the
few ziphiids that can be readily identified
at sea. Older males, in particular, are
often heavily scarred from the teeth of
other males and from bites by cookie-
cutter sharks. The two teeth erupt
only in males and can be

male

female

seen protruding from the tip of the lower jaw, even when the mouth is closed; they sometimes have stalked barnacles growing on them. Cuvier's beaked whales strand more than any other member of the beaked whale family.

Where to look
Widely distributed from the tropics to cool temperate waters worldwide, Cuvier's beaked whales seem to have very specific habitat requirements – deep waters on the steepest portion of the continental slope. It is difficult to predict sightings, but a few of the hotspots where they are sometimes seen on whale-watch trips include the Bay of Biscay, the Canary Islands, the Mediterranean and Hawaii.

Baird's Beaked Whale

Berardius bairdii

ID FACT FILE

OTHER NAMES
Giant bottlenose
whale, four-
toothed whale.
MAXIMUM LENGTH
12.8 metres.
MAXIMUM WEIGHT
12 tonnes.
FIELD ID
Large size; long,
dark grey, spindle-
shaped body;
extensive scarring
on older animals;
small fin two-
thirds of the way
along back;
prominent,
bulbous forehead
sloping to long
beak; anterior
teeth may appear
white in bright
sunlight; tightly-
packed groups.
DIET
Squid and fish.

BREEDING
Calves every
3 years or more;
gestation possibly
as long as 17
months.

The largest member of the family, Baird's
beaked whale is very similar to Arnoux's
beaked whale. These two species are
unusual in having four teeth which erupt
in both males and females: one large pair
at the tip of the protruding lower jaw and
a smaller pair just behind them. Baird's
beaked whale was discovered in 1882
when researcher Leonhard Stejneger
picked up a four-toothed skull on Bering
Island. He published his discovery the
following year and named the new species
after his colleague, Spencer Baird, who
had just been appointed Secretary of the
Smithsonian Institution. Like other
members of the family, Baird's beaked
whales are deep divers. They can probably
hold their breath for an hour or more, but
most dives last around half an hour;

they are believed to reach depths of at least 1,000 metres on a regular basis. They are usually shy of vessels and difficult to approach, but can be active at the surface and have been observed spyhopping and breaching. The status of Baird's beaked whales is uncertain, but the world population is possibly in the order of a few tens of thousands.

Where to look

Deep temperate and sub-arctic waters in the North Pacific, especially around submarine escarpments and seamounts. Baird's beaked whales are rarely found close to shore, unless the continental shelf is exceptionally narrow. They have been hunted by the Japanese for centuries and 50–60 are still killed every year under a government quota system, mainly in the waters off the Boso Peninsula, near Tokyo, and off Hokkaido Island in the north.

Arnoux's Beaked Whale

Berardius arnuxii

Arnoux's beaked whale is a very poorly-known whale, resembling Baird's beaked whale so closely that for many years it was uncertain whether Baird's represented a geographically isolated form of Arnoux's. But recent genetic studies seem to have settled the dispute in favour of two separate species. The main visible difference appears to be in size: Arnoux's is slightly smaller than Baird's. The two beaked whales would probably be indistinguishable at sea, although their ranges do not appear to overlap and it is highly unlikely that they would ever come into contact with one another. They are among the least sexually dimorphic members of the family – both males and females have erupted teeth and look remarkably similar. Named after a French surgeon, M. Arnoux, who presented the first skull to the Paris Museum of Natural History in 1846, Arnoux's beaked whale is usually shy and difficult to observe.

Where to look

Arnoux's beaked whales appear to inhabit vast areas of the southern hemisphere, from the Antarctic to southern Brazil, South Georgia, South Africa, New Zealand and Australia. Most records are south of 40°S from temperate to Antarctic waters. They are not known in the tropics. There is no information on abundance but, unlike its northern hemisphere relative, Arnoux's beaked whale is not taken by commercial whalers.

Northern Bottlenose Whale

Hyperoodon ampullatus

One of the three most-watched members of the family (along with Cuvier's beaked whale and Baird's beaked whale), the northern bottlenose whale is a curious animal and frequently approaches stationary or slow-moving boats. Its most distinctive feature is its huge bulbous

forehead, which is particularly prominent in older males. There are two teeth at the tip of the lower jaw (erupting in males only) which are sometimes covered in stalked barnacles. Capable of diving to depths of 1,500 metres, it can remain submerged for over an hour. Hunted more than any other beaked whale, it has now been protected for more than 25 years.

Where to look

Lives in the cooler waters of the North Atlantic, mainly north of the Iberian Peninsula in the east and Nova Scotia in the west. It prefers deep water, especially beyond the continental shelf and over submarine canyons. Little is known about its seasonal movements – for instance, it appears to be present year-round in the Gully (a submarine canyon off Nova Scotia) but only during the summer in the southern Bay of Biscay.

Southern Bottlenose Whale
Hyperoodon planifrons

The southern bottlenose whale is quite poorly known. It lives far from shipping lanes, and has never been heavily exploited, so most information comes from strandings and incidental observations by researchers studying other species. It is not particularly difficult to identify at sea, although it does look similar to Arnoux's beaked whale from a distance and the two species have almost identical ranges.

The chocolatey yellow-brown colour is believed to be caused by a thin layer of diatoms (single-celled algae) as well as by natural pigmentation. They are usually found in small groups (one to four individuals is typical), although up to 20 have been observed together. Abundance estimates for the region south of the Antarctic Convergence in summer suggest a population of about 500,000.

ID FACT FILE

OTHER NAMES
Antarctic bottlenosed whale, flathead.

MAXIMUM LENGTH
7.5 metres.

MAXIMUM WEIGHT
Unknown.

FIELD ID
(Male only) Long, robust body; dark, yellow-brown upperside, light underside; can look white at sea; bulbous melon, pale and squared-off; stubby beak; tiny teeth at tip; visible, bushy blow; prominent, falcate fin.

DIET
Squid, some fish and benthic invertebrates.

BREEDING
Possibly calves every 2-3 years; gestation may be about 12 months.

Where to look

Found throughout the cold, deep waters of the southern hemisphere, from the Antarctic ice edge to about 30°S (with occasional sightings further north, especially in winter). Limited evidence suggests that there are seasonal movements, at least in some populations: the highest density, for instance, occurs during summer within about 100 kilometres of the Antarctic ice edge.

Pygmy Killer Whale
Feresa attenuata

ID FACT FILE

OTHER NAMES
Lesser killer
whale, slender
blackfish,
slender pilot
whale.
MAXIMUM LENGTH
2.6 metres.
MAXIMUM WEIGHT
170 kilograms.
FIELD ID
Robust, dark-
coloured body;
slightly paler grey
sides, white
patch on
underside; dark
dorsal cape
visible in some
light conditions;
rounded head
with no beak and
white lips; some
individuals have
white chin;
prominent
falcate fin.
DIET
Mostly fish and
squid.
BREEDING
Calving interval
and gestation
period unknown.

Although no bigger than a dolphin itself, the pygmy killer whale is known to attack other small cetaceans in the wild and has been quite aggressive towards other species and even people in captivity. Although it is widely distributed, it is not particularly well known. There are reports of bow-riding and wake-riding, but it tends to be less active than most oceanic dolphins and usually avoids boats. Schools often swim abreast in long 'chorus lines' and, when alarmed, bunch together – often leaping clear of the water in their determination to rush away. When viewed at close range, it is possible to see a distinctive white chin on some individuals and the white lips that are common in this species. It is similar in size to many oceanic dolphins, though is most likely to be confused with the

similar-looking melon-headed whale: generally
speaking, if a small number of animals are seen
together (fewer than 50) they are more likely to be
pygmy killer whales.

Where to look
Found worldwide in deep, offshore waters mainly in
the tropics and sub-tropics but also in warm
temperate regions, the pygmy killer whale rarely
occurs close to shore except around oceanic islands.
Small numbers are drowned in fishing nets and
caught up in drive fisheries in Japan, Sri Lanka and
elsewhere, and in several countries (especially in
Asia) it is harpooned opportunistically.

Melon-headed Whale

Peponocephala electra

There seems to have been some
confusion over the melon-headed
whale's common name. The scientific
word *Peponocephala* was believed to
mean 'melon-headed' – 'pepo' was
thought to be Latin for 'melon' – and so
was used to describe the distinctively-
shaped, pointed head of this species.
But it has since transpired that 'pepo'
probably means 'pumpkin' – so, strictly-
speaking, it should be the pumpkin-
headed whale instead. Despite its wide
distribution, it is infrequently
encountered at sea except at certain
hotspots such as the
Maldives, Cebu
Island in the
Philippines,
Hawaii and off
the east coast of
Australia. It often creates a
lot of spray as it surfaces, and
frequently changes direction
underwater, making it difficult to see in
any detail. Confusion is most likely with
the pygmy killer whale, which is very
similar in appearance: generally
speaking, if there are several hundred
animals together they are more likely to
be melon-headed whales. Also, unlike
pygmy killer whales, they are
sometimes encountered in mixed
schools with Fraser's dolphins.

Where to look

Mainly found in deep, sub-tropical and tropical waters worldwide, the melon-headed whale is most common between about 20°N and 20°S. It is sometimes observed in temperate regions, though these are probably strays travelling in warm currents. Melon-headed whales are usually encountered offshore, and rarely venture close to shore except around oceanic islands or where the water is deep. Some drown in fishing nets and they are harpooned throughout their range.

False Killer Whale

Pseudorca crassidens

ID FACT FILE

OTHER NAMES
False pilot whale,
pseudorca.

MAXIMUM LENGTH
6 metres.

MAXIMUM WEIGHT
2 tonnes.

FIELD ID
Relatively long
and slender
body; uniformly
dark except for
light areas on
throat and chest;
slender, rounded
or conical head
with no beak;
melon overhangs
tip of lower jaw
(adult male only);
unique 'elbow'
on flippers;
prominent,
falcate fin; fairly
acrobatic.

DIET
Mostly fish and
squid, known to
attack other
cetaceans.

BREEDING
Calving interval
possibly up to 7
years; gestation
14–16 months.

The false killer whale can look rather
menacing and has been known to attack
groups of small cetaceans. On one
occasion it even attacked a nursery school
of sperm whales and, on another, killed a
humpback whale calf. Yet it is often seen
in the company of bottlenose dolphins
and, in captivity, shows less aggression
than its smaller relative the pygmy killer
whale. One of the largest members of the
dolphin family, in many ways it behaves
more like an oceanic dolphin: it leaps
high into the air, makes rapid turns
underwater, and even rides the bow-
waves of boats and ships. It is a fast and
active swimmer, often lifting its entire
head and much of its body out of the
water when it surfaces. False killer
whales seem to be susceptible to
stranding, and sometimes come ashore in
huge numbers (more than 800 in one
exceptional case). They normally occur in
groups of around 20 animals, but it is not
unusual for many smaller groups to travel
together. They are unpopular with
fishermen and have a reputation for

stealing fish such as tuna from baited lines. The
common name refers to a similarity in skull
morphology with the killer whale, rather than a
similarity in external appearance.

Where to look
Widely distributed in tropical, sub-tropical and
warm temperate waters worldwide (including
enclosed seas such as the Mediterranean and Red
Sea). False killer whales prefer deep water and,
except around oceanic islands, are normally
encountered offshore. Small numbers drown in
fishing nets and are hunted for food or by fishermen
who regard them as competitors. A few are also
captured for marine parks.

Short-finned Pilot Whale

Globicephala macrorhynchus

ID FACT FILE

OTHER NAMES
Pacific pilot whale, blackfish, pothead whale.
MAXIMUM LENGTH
7.2 metres (male), 5.1 metres (female).
MAXIMUM WEIGHT
Possibly 4 tonnes.
FIELD ID
Long, stocky body; black, grey or dark brown; pale saddle-patch behind fin (variable); large, rounded head with bulbous melon; may be light diagonal stripe behind each eye; no visible beak; shorter flippers than long-finned; low, broad-based fin far forward on body (sweeps backward).
DIET
Mainly squid, some fish and octopuses.
BREEDING
Calves every 5–8 years; gestation 15-16 months.

Pilot whales are among the largest members of the dolphin family. Their name originates from an early theory (probably not true) that a school is piloted or led by one particular leader. Both long-finned and short-finned pilot whales exhibit striking sexual dimorphism in size: males are considerably longer than females and have a more pronounced melon and much larger dorsal fin. They are highly social animals, typically living in small groups (10–20 individuals in long-finned and 15–90 in short-finned), which often come together to form much larger gatherings. As in killer whale pods, these close-knit families stay together for life and most individuals never leave (although males mate with females from other groups to avoid inbreeding). Females continue to ovulate until their late thirties and may still be lactating in their late forties; they probably live well into their sixties. Limited estimates of abundance suggest a population of some 160,000 in the eastern tropical Pacific and 30,000–50,000 in southern Japan. Several hundred short-finned pilot whales are killed annually in Japan and the Caribbean, and they are hunted in Indonesia and Sri Lanka.

Where to look

The short-finned pilot whale prefers warm water
and is found worldwide in the tropics and sub-
tropics and in warm temperate regions. It is
common in the Canary Islands and occurs around
Madeira and the Azores, but is absent from the
Mediterranean. There is little, but probably some,
overlap in range with the long-finned pilot whale –
mainly in temperate waters of the Atlantic, in the
Pacific off the coast of Peru, Tasmania and the
south-east coast of Australia, and off South Africa.

Tucuxi
Sotalia fluviatilis

There are two sub-species of tucuxi
(pronounced tookooshee): a relatively
small one found in lakes and rivers, and a
considerably larger one in the sea. The
riverine form has been studied in some
detail, but less is
known about the
marine form.

Despite its large riverine population, it is
a member of the family Delphinidae and
is not closely related to the 'true' river
dolphins (although, in the Amazon Basin,
it is not unusual to see tucuxis feeding in
the company of Amazon river dolphins).
It is often referred to simply as 'Sotalia',
which is the first part of its scientific
name. At first glance it looks rather like a
small bottlenose dolphin – and
sometimes behaves like one, too. Tucuxis
are fairly active at the surface and can be
seen breaching, spyhopping and
splashing; they are not known to bow-
ride, but will sometimes play in the wake
of passing boats and ships. As well as

hunting, incidental capture in fishing nets and
conflicts with fisheries, the damming of the Amazon,
mangrove degradation and coastal pollution are all
threats.

Where to look
The tucuxi is found in warm, shallow coastal waters
of north-eastern South America and eastern Central
America (from Nicaragua to Florianópolis in Brazil)
and throughout much of the Amazon River basin.
Coastal populations are most common in estuaries
and large bays, while riverine ones are found as far
as 2,500 kilometres up the Amazon. They appear to
be fairly common over much of their range.

Spinner Dolphin

Stenella longirostris

ID FACT FILE

OTHER NAMES
Long-snouted
spinner,
longsnout,
rollover, long-
beaked dolphin.

MAXIMUM LENGTH
2.4 metres.

MAXIMUM WEIGHT
90 kilograms.

FIELD ID
Slender body;
three-part colour
pattern; long,
narrow beak with
dark tip; upper
jaw grey, lower
jaw often cream;
dark stripe from
eye to flipper;
gently-sloping
melon; tall fin can
be slightly falcate
or erect (leans
forward in some
individuals);
performs high,
spinning leaps.

DIET
Fish, squid and
crustaceans.

BREEDING
Calves every 3
years; gestation
just over 10
months.

One of the most acrobatic of all dolphins, the spinner was named for its incredibly high spinning leaps. It can spin round on its longitudinal axis as many as seven times before splashing back into the water. No other cetacean shows so much variation in appearance from one region to another and there are currently four recognised sub-species, differing greatly in body shape, size, colour and even behaviour. The colour pattern in most regions is basically three-part, albeit with considerable regional differences, consisting of a dark-grey cape, light-grey sides and white underside. Numbers were reduced significantly by tuna fishing in the eastern tropical Pacific (which has been responsible for killing more dolphins in the past 35 years than any other human activity). Fortunately, public outrage has forced the authorities to introduce new rules and regulations, which include releasing dolphins from the nets when they are captured, and the scale of the slaughter has dropped to thousands (rather than hundreds of thousands) of deaths a year. However, the population of eastern spinners is still probably less than half its original size.

Where to look
The spinner is found mainly in tropical and sub-tropical waters worldwide, although it sometimes occurs in warm temperate waters as well. Depending on the sub-species, it can be seen in shallow water close to shore, around oceanic islands or far out to sea. Many spinners are hunted or drowned in gill nets every year, especially in Australia and Asia. Despite all the threats, it is still fairly common in some parts of its range.

Clymene Dolphin
Stenella clymene

ID FACT FILE

OTHER NAMES
Short-snouted
spinner dolphin,
Senegal dolphin,
helmet dolphin.
MAXIMUM LENGTH
2 metres.
MAXIMUM WEIGHT
80 kilograms.
FIELD ID
Relatively small,
fairly robust
body; three-toned
colour pattern;
dark grey or
black cape dips
below fin; long
beak with black
tip, lips and
'moustache';
pale grey stripe
from eye to
flipper; dark,
slender flippers;
prominent,
slightly falcate or
triangular fin.
DIET
Fish and squid.
BREEDING
Calving interval
and gestation
period unknown.

For many years the clymene dolphin, or short-snouted spinner dolphin as it is often called, was considered to be one of the many variations of the long-snouted spinner. The two animals sometimes associate with one another and, like the spinner, the clymene has a three-toned colouration: a dark grey cape, lighter grey sides, and a white underside. Some populations even spin longitudinally when breaching, although not as frequently or as elaborately as spinners. But the clymene dolphin (pronounced cly-mee-nee) was officially classified as a separate species in 1981. There is considerable overlap in range between the two species in the Atlantic, and they can be difficult to tell apart at sea. The clymene dolphin is usually seen in groups of up to 50 animals (although

several hundred have been observed together).
Schools may be segregated by sex, and possibly
age, since several mass strandings have consisted
almost entirely of females or males. It is a keen
bow-rider and will go out of its way to accompany
a boat or ship, yet remains one of the least-known
oceanic dolphins.

Where to look
Found in warm temperate, sub-tropical and tropical
waters of the Atlantic Ocean, the clymene dolphin
occurs mainly in deep waters offshore. It appears
to be absent from the Mediterranean, but details
of its distribution are lacking. Little is also known
about its abundance. Some hunting takes place
in the Caribbean and it is caught incidentally in
fishing nets in many parts of its range, especially
in West Africa.

Striped Dolphin
Stenella coeruleoalba

ID FACT FILE

OTHER NAMES
Streaker,
whitebelly.

MAXIMUM LENGTH
2.7 metres.

MAXIMUM WEIGHT
160 kilograms.

FIELD ID
Fairly robust
body; bluish-grey
upperside, pale
grey sides and
tail stock, white
or pinkish
underside; long,
dark side stripe;
pale shoulder
blaze sweeping
up towards fin;
dark stripe from
eye to flipper;
prominent beak;
dark, prominent
fin.

DIET
Squid and fish
(lanternfish a
favourite in some
areas).

BREEDING
Calves every 4
years; gestation
12–13 months.

Striped dolphins are highly conspicuous animals, seeming to spend an inordinate amount of their time in the air. Their acrobatic repertoire includes high breaches, belly-flops, chin-slaps, back somersaults, tail spins, and upside-down porpoising. They also have a unique behaviour, called 'roto-tailing', which involves leaping into a high arc and then rapidly rotating the tail before re-entering the water. Their distinctive stripes, and the speed at which they swim, prompted fishermen to call them 'streakers'. In some parts of the world they readily approach boats, but they are more wary and do not bow-ride in the eastern tropical Pacific where, until quite recently, considerable numbers were killed by the tuna-fishing industry. Known to live to the ripe old age of nearly 60 years, they are fairly well known and several different populations have been studied in detail.

Where to look

Found worldwide, striped dolphins live mainly in tropical, sub-tropical and warm temperate waters – although they occur as far north as southern Greenland and Iceland. Despite large numbers being killed incidentally by a pelagic drift-net fishery, they are probably the commonest cetaceans in the Mediterranean Sea. Usually encountered offshore, they are hunted in some regions of the world, especially in the Japanese drive fishery.

Pantropical Spotted Dolphin

Stenella attenuata

ID FACT FILE

OTHER NAMES
Spotted dolphin,
spotter.

MAXIMUM LENGTH
2.6 metres.

MAXIMUM WEIGHT
120 kilograms.

FIELD ID
Slender,
elongated body
(variable); dark
grey cape, lighter
underside; most
adults heavily
spotted; long,
narrow beak with
white tip and
lips; thick, dark
stripe from beak
to flipper; tall,
strongly falcate
fin.

DIET
Squid and fish,
some
crustaceans.

BREEDING
Calves every 2–4
years; gestation
11–12 months.

Tuna-fishing operations in the eastern
tropical Pacific killed so many
pantropical spotted dolphins in the
1960s, 1970s and 1980s that the regional
population declined by as much as 75 per
cent. Literally millions of the animals
were killed, along with huge numbers of
other dolphin species. New laws and
release techniques have reduced the
level of the slaughter dramatically, but it
has still not been stopped altogether. It is
still unclear why the dolphins associate
with tuna – it might increase foraging
efficiency or provide better protection
from predators. Adults are usually
covered in white spots, which fuse and
fade to a medium-grey as they get older,
but newborn calves are unspotted.
However, there is a lot of variation in the
appearance of individuals within a
population and between populations in
different parts of the world. Three sub-
species are currently recognised: one
living mainly in coastal waters of the

eastern Pacific tends to be larger, more spotted and more robust. Pantropical spotted dolphins spend a lot of time in the air and youngsters, in particular, can make some impressively high vertical leaps.

Where to look

Found worldwide in tropical and some sub-tropical waters of the Atlantic, Pacific and Indian Oceans, the pantropical spotted dolphin occurs both inshore and offshore. It is most abundant nearer the equator, but is known as far north as 40°N and as far south as 40°S. Although hunted in many parts of the world and caught incidentally in fishing nets, it is still surprisingly abundant and the world population is estimated to be at least three million.

Atlantic Spotted Dolphin
Stenella frontalis

There are so many variations in the
markings of spotted dolphins
that their taxonomy has
puzzled experts for a
long time. But
the Atlantic
spotted dolphin is one of just two
currently recognised species. Most adults
have dark spots on the underside and
light spots on the sides and back, but
some are not spotted at all and others are
so heavily spotted they appear almost
white from a distance. Young animals
have no spots but these begin to appear
as they grow older. The Atlantic spotted
dolphin is difficult to tell apart from the
very similar pantropical spotted dolphin,
but the distinctive diagonal shoulder
blaze that sweeps up through the cape
towards the dorsal fin is diagnostic. One
particular population of Atlantic spotted
dolphins on Little Bahama Bank, north
of the Bahamas, has been studied in
great detail since the 1970s, but the
species is less well known elsewhere in
the Atlantic.

Where to look

As its name suggests, the Atlantic spotted
dolphin is found in the Atlantic – both
North and South – in warm temperate,
sub-tropical and tropical waters. The
range extends from about 50°N to 25°S,
but it does not appear to include the